THE THAMES IRON WORKS 1837–1912:
A MAJOR SHIPBUILDER ON THE THAMES

Daniel Harrison

Published by MOLA [Museum of London Archaeology]

Copyright © Crossrail Limited 2015

A CIP catalogue record for this book is available from the British Library

Production and design by Tracy Wellman

Reprographics by Andy Chopping

Copy editing by Wendy Sherlock

General editing by Sue Hirst/Susan M Wright

Front cover: the launch of Japanese battleship *Shikishima* on 1 November 1898 (National Maritime Museum, Greenwich, London, C6851)

Printed by Henry Ling Ltd at the Dorset Press, an ISO 14001 certified printer

MIX
Paper from
responsible sources
FSC® C013985

CONTRIBUTORS

Principal author	**Daniel Harrison**
Building material	Ian M Betts
Accessioned finds	Lyn Blackmore
Leather	Beth Richardson
Timber identification	Karen Stewart
Timber boat	Damian Goodburn
Graphics	Carlos Lemos, Paul Thrale
Photography	Andy Chopping, Maggie Cox
Project manager	Elaine Eastbury
Post-excavation manager	Lucy Whittingham
Editor	Sue Hirst

CONTENTS

FIGURES

TABLES

SUMMARY

The Thames Iron Works and Shipbuilding Company (with its predecessors, 1837–1912) was one of the great private enterprises of the Victorian age of industrialism. It launched, from its slipways at the mouth of the River Lea, many of the most famous and exemplary warships of the era including HMS *Warrior* (1860), the first ocean-going all-iron warship. Flourishing in the mid 19th century as a builder of iron ships, it provided for both the Royal Navy as well as foreign navies, who flocked to the banks of the Lea to furnish their fleets with the most technologically advanced vessels available. The shipyard also catered for the international merchant marine and its name became known both nationally and internationally as a byword for modernity and quality of craftsmanship. In addition to its prowess as a shipbuilder, the Thames Iron Works was involved in the construction of some of the definitive civil engineering works of the era.

Recent archaeological excavations at the launch-site of Crossrail tunnelling machines on the Limmo Peninsula have afforded a glimpse of this vanished industry and an investigation of several important components of the yard, including engineering workshops, a furnace, a mast house and mould loft building, and a slipway. Along with a discussion of the archaeological findings, this book aims to present a historical framework for the development of the Thames Iron Works and to place it within the larger context of London and the contemporary shipbuilding industry. The development of the Thames Iron Works closely parallels that of the east London suburb of West Ham, and also London more generally, from the 1830s to the first decade of the 20th century. During its lifetime, the Thames Iron Works was affected by prevailing national economic conditions and impacted significantly on the lives of thousands employed in the area and their dependents. In response to economic hardship and strike action in the latter part of the 19th century, the ironworks became an early proponent of improving employment practice and also introduced various social clubs and societies. One of these clubs, which has lived on till today, is still referred to as the 'Irons' – West Ham United Football Club.

ACKNOWLEDGEMENTS

MOLA would like to thank Crossrail Limited, in particular Jay Carver, for enabling this project at Limmo Peninsula. We would like to extend our thanks to David Shepherd (Crossrail) and Noel Curtis and Bruno Guillaume (Dragados Sisk). The author would also like to thank the staff of the archives visited for their kind assistance and interest in the project, in particular Penny Allen at Royal Museums Greenwich.

MOLA staff who worked on the evaluation and targeted watching brief were Tanya Bowie, Sasathorn Charoenphan, Robert Hartle, Sam Pfizenmaier, David Sankey, Chris Spence and Paul Thrale. Other key staff were Virgil Yendell (geoarchaeology), Liz Goodman (conservation), Mark Burch, Moises Hernandez Cordero, Neville Constantine and Catherine Drew (geomatics), and Portia Askew who helped gather the documentary evidence. George Dennis was the MOLA senior contract manager.

The author is grateful to Paul Thrale for his research on the slipway and illustrated reconstruction, and also to Greater London Industrial Archaeology Society (GLIAS) specialists, Malcolm Tucker and Robert Carr, for their comments on the furnace and to David Cranstone for further discussion on the slag deposits and type of furnace.

FOREWORD

Marilyn Palmer, Professor of Industrial Archaeology, University of Leicester

Industrial archaeology came into being in the 1950s in order to record and preserve, as far as possible, the surviving standing remains of Britain's Industrial Revolution. Excavation played a very small role and most of the building recording work was carried out by volunteers. By the 1980s, the drastic curtailment of traditional British industry such as textile manufacture, coal mining and iron working meant that volunteers could no longer cope with the amount of recording that was necessary and professional bodies began to take an interest, mainly in standing industrial monuments. However, it was perhaps the advent of professional archaeological contract units in the 1990s that changed the nature of industrial archaeology, since their work involved the excavation of multi-period sites in advance of development rather than individual research excavations. It was finally recognised that the excavation of industrial sites could add to the understanding of the role played by industrialisation, its social consequences and the resulting changes in the landscape.

Large-scale excavation of such sites has become more frequent in the 21st century with massive redevelopment taking place in city centres, as new industries take the place of the old, while possible contamination posed by traditional industries has led to wholesale site clearance. Whereas the important work carried out by volunteers from the earliest days of industrial archaeology is still valuable, only the professional archaeological units have the skills and resources to undertake the kind of research and excavation described in this book, and they could only do this with the cooperation and financial assistance of the developers involved. Railway construction in a city like London, densely occupied over centuries, has created valuable opportunities for learning more about its past and MOLA has already published the results of work on such undertakings, for example Emma Dwyer's book, *The impact of the railways in the East End 1835–2010: historical archaeology from the London Overground East London line*. The Crossrail project has, of course, created opportunities to explore the city at greater depth, as demonstrated in this book, where the need to dig large shafts for the huge boring machines, which have become familiar thanks to television programmes, has enabled archaeologists to reveal the physical remains of one of the largest shipyards on the Thames and the one from which HMS *Warrior* was launched in 1860. Some of the photographs in the book indicate the close working proximity of the archaeologists and engineers on the site, the linings for the shafts clearly visible while the archaeological recording is progressing.

The book demonstrates the essence of archaeological work on the historic past, where maps and documents can be used to great effect in conjunction with excavation of subsurface remains. The various trenches dug by the archaeologists on the Limmo Peninsula could be correlated with a sequence of historic maps in order to give them some idea of the features they were likely to encounter, since these are often difficult to recognise without their superstructure. The archaeological material answered some of the questions raised about the processes carried out on the site, which are not always dealt with in documentary sources. Wrought iron, used for the plating of ships until the development of armour plate in the 1880s, was derived mainly from scrap iron, and the analysis of slag from the puddling furnaces, the bases of some of which were excavated, confirmed the existence of such structures. More spectacular were the excavations of the massive slipways which were used to launch the huge ships produced by the Thames Iron Works, as well as the foundations of the mast house and mould loft. It is very difficult otherwise to convey to a generation accustomed to industrial activity focusing on microchips and computer software the vast scale of much 19th-century industry, but the sheer size of the excavated features illustrated in this book certainly helps in a very graphic way.

The archaeological work is part of a well-researched historical framework, which incorporates discussion of the labour relations in the ironworks and the social activities of those employed there. Industrial archaeologists in the past have tended to ignore the fact that structures were built and artefacts manufactured by people, concentrating instead on the technological processes. It is fascinating to read that one of the social clubs founded in this works eventually became the Irons, West Ham United Football Club, and perhaps even more surprising to see a photograph of their operatic society dressed for a performance of the *Pirates of Penzance*. This is a well-balanced account of an important shipyard on the Thames which took up the challenge of the transition from wooden ships to massive iron-clad steamships for the Admiralty and the merchant marine in the period leading up until the First World War. It is salutary to realise that shipbuilding was not just a feature of the economy of the north-east of England and the Clyde, but played a major part in the development of the banks of the Thames east of the Port of London.

CHAPTER 1

INTRODUCTION

1.1 The site in West Ham

The Thames in London is now a relatively quiet river. Freight and passenger shipping withdrew, along with much of the previous heavy industry fronting the Thames, in the middle of the last century, leaving behind the converted wharves and place names. A notable absence, however, is any visible evidence of shipbuilding. Shipyards were a major feature of London's economy but have left little trace.

Peaking in the 19th century, London was a world centre for shipbuilding, and enterprises could be found from the estuary as far upstream as Chiswick, in Hounslow (formerly Middlesex). Shipyards proliferated on the banks of Millwall, Blackwall, the Isle of Dogs and Cubitt Town, all in Tower Hamlets (formerly Middlesex),[1] producing wooden ships and boats up to the mid 19th century, and then great ships of iron and later steel. The shipyards worked alongside the naval dockyards and, with some of the great engineering names of the era such as Penn and Maudsley supplying machinery, the industrial powerhouse of the Thames became a leading innovator of the age. The British Admiralty placed over half of their outside orders with private shipyards on the Thames in the years leading up to 1850.[2] 'Blackwall fashion' became a byword for quality and modernity, and foreign powers looked to London to furnish their own developing navies with ships.

Now the river by night is brightened at points by the brilliant lights of wealthy residential developments, though once downstream of the glittering towers around Canary Wharf much of the river is dark. On a patch of ground opposite The O$_2$ dome, however, a little more than a hundred years ago the night-time river would have reflected scores of people working on a giant shape, red sparks flying from the riveters as they worked to finish the largest ship ever launched on the Thames, the battleship HMS *Thunderer* (Fig 1; Chapter 3.3). The ship was the largest in the world at the time of launching in February 1911, and it was launched not directly into the Thames but into the River Lea. This patch of ground contained by the final curves of the Lea (Fig 2) was the home of the Thames Iron Works, one of the pioneers of the Victorian age of industrialism and one of the most enduring of the iron shipbuilding enterprises in London. At its peak, the Thames Iron Works occupied both banks of the Lea, the only shipbuilder operating in the counties of both Middlesex and Essex. The launch of HMS *Thunderer* was, however, a final flourish; by the end of 1912 the Thames Iron Works had closed.

Fig 1 HMS *Thunderer* at anchor at Spithead on completion, 1912

(Imperial War Museum, Q21854)

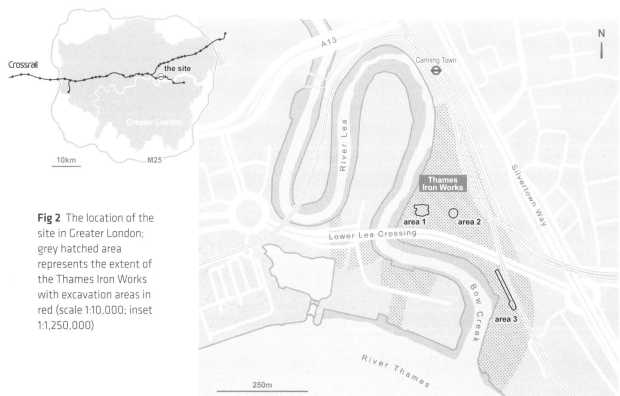

Fig 2 The location of the site in Greater London; grey hatched area represents the extent of the Thames Iron Works with excavation areas in red (scale 1:10,000; inset 1:1,250,000)

The rise and fall of the Thames Iron Works parallels closely the urban and industrial development of the east London suburb of West Ham, in Newham (formerly Essex), and also reflects industrial and economic trends of both London and the nation during the period from the 1830s to the first decade of the 20th century (Fig 3). The ironworks mirrored prevailing economic conditions, witnessing both years of boom and of crisis. Fluctuations in shipbuilding and later civil engineering output at the yard directly affected the thousands employed in the area and their dependents. Times of extreme hardship, together with the general decline of Thames shipbuilding following a major banking crisis of 1866, prompted dock and shipyard workers to join strikes across London over the following years and led to the increased unionisation of workers as part of a more general social movement. Out of the industrial strife, the ironworks came to be a leading proponent of change in employment practice, revolutionising workers' rights such as the introduction of the eight-hour day and instituting a form of profit-sharing dubbed the 'good fellowship system'. The ironworks, under its final owner Arnold Hills, also introduced various social enterprises in the guise of clubs and societies, aimed at improving worker-employer relations and workers' quality of life. One of these clubs lived on beyond the demise of the ironworks as West Ham United Football Club, still known as the 'Irons' (Fig 96).

Fig 3 The Thames Iron Works in 1895, view looking north
(Newham Heritage Service)

Fig 4 The Thames Iron Works mast house *c* 1863, view looking east (HMS *Warrior* Preservation Trust)

1.2 About this book

This book presents an account of the development of the Thames Iron Works and Shipbuilding Company from humble beginnings as Ditchburn and Mare in 1837 to the peak of the iron shipbuilding industry in London in the 1850s and to its ultimate closure in 1912. Beginning in 2009, archaeological work undertaken by the Museum of London Archaeology (MOLA) on the site of the former Thames Iron Works, as part of the Crossrail project, has afforded a rare glimpse of a vanished industry. In 2011 and 2012, major works took place at the Limmo Peninsula (probably a corruption of Lea Mouth) where two large shafts were dug for Crossrail tunnel-boring machines (Fig 2, areas 1 and 2). Work also took place to the south at Instone Wharf where a facility was constructed for storing spoil generated by the tunnelling and then loading it on to barges for transportation (Fig 2, area 3). This book aims to describe the remains uncovered in the archaeological investigations and to place them in the wider context of the Thames Iron Works.

Chapter 2 provides an outline of shipbuilding as it was undertaken in the early days of the shipyard which became the Thames Iron Works, in the period of transition from wood and sail to iron and steam, followed by an account of the raw materials and industrial processes involved in iron shipbuilding. Chapter 3 presents a brief history of the ironworks and the owners, and includes a discussion of some of the ships built there. The archaeological investigations are detailed in Chapter 4 and the structures found related to the known development of the ironworks. Chapter 5 discusses labour relations and social change in the area as demonstrated by the history of the ironworks, with a concluding Chapter 6 discussing the area of the site after the demise of the Thames Iron Works.

County names in the text refer to historic counties. Weights and measures quoted in the text are, where appropriate, in the units used before metrication (feet and inches, abbreviated to ft and in) along with conversions (1ft equals 0.305m; 12in to 1ft). An acre is 0.4 hectare (abbreviated to ha) or alternatively one hectare equals about 2.5 acres. A pound in weight (abbreviated to lb) equals 0.45kg. One metric tonne (or 1000kg) is equivalent to 0.98 long ton or 1 long ton (2240 pounds) is equivalent to 1.016 metric tonnes. One hundredweight (abbreviated to cwt) equals 112lb or 50.80kg and 20cwt equals 1 long ton. In British gravitational units, one ton-force is equivalent to 8896 newtons (abbreviated to N).

Sums of money are quoted in the text as cited in £, s and d, where 12 pence (d) made one shilling (s) and 20 shillings (or 240d) a pound (£), since modern equivalents would be misleading; however, where appropriate sums have been converted for specific years with respect to values current in 2005.[3] A sovereign is a gold coin with a nominal value of £1. The gold content for a sovereign was set by Parliament in 1816 at 0.234 troy ounces or 7.322g and this weight remains almost constant to the present day.

The paper and digital archives, together with the finds from the site, are publicly accessible in the archive of the Museum of London, where they are held under the site code XRW10. They can be consulted by prior arrangement at the London Archaeological Archive and Research Centre (LAARC), Mortimer Wheeler House, 46 Eagle Wharf Road, London N1 7ED.[4]

The basic unit of reference in the site archive is the context number. These are grouped into the land-use entities referred to in this report as Building (B) and Structure (S), which are generally numbered sequentially. Accession numbers given to certain artefacts are shown thus: <10>.

1.3 Historical sources used

The company records and archives of the private shipbuilding concerns on the Thames have been largely lost in the century that has passed since their final chapter.[5] This is certainly true for the Thames Iron Works, for which there are very few contemporary documents available for the period before the 1890s. Also, many of these documents are journalism of noteworthy events or accounts of the yard by external visitors, which, while often colourful and offering intriguing insight on life in the shipyard, were written by gentlemen with little technical expertise or real knowledge of the workings of the yards and have to be treated with caution. Later documentary sources, maps and photographs, however, have helped us to understand the development of the yard over time and to date the archaeology. This book makes use of the few documents that do survive. The most useful of these was the *Thames Iron Works Gazette* (*TIWG*), which has proved enlightening in every aspect of trying to understand the archaeology of the site (Fig 5). The *TIWG* was an extraordinary document produced quarterly under Arnold Hills's direction (above, 1.1) from January 1895 to 1911 and was a somewhat incongruous mix of works newsletter, technical journal, general interest publication and also sporting and societies almanac. It included serialised material on various topics related to the ironworks, such as the history of the unions at the works. Perhaps the most useful of these serials to any study of the development of

Fig 5 The *Thames Iron Works Gazette*, no. 50, May 1911; the *TIWG* often included poetry which Hills no doubt hoped would edify and educate the readers (Science Museum Library/ Science & Society Picture Library, MS 616/2)

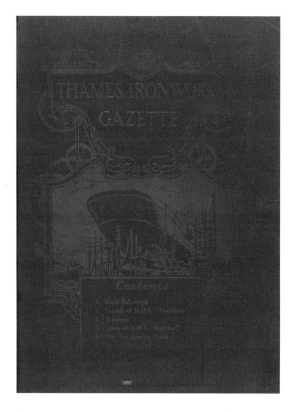

the works are the 'Reminiscences'. These start from the first issue and take the form of primarily first-hand accounts of the works over a number of decades beginning with the 1840s. They were penned by George Colby Mackrow, an employee of the firm who rose to become head of shipbuilding and the Thames Iron Works's lead naval architect. Mackrow was ironworks man and boy. Having tried his hand at coopering, silversmithing and optical instrument making, he found shipbuilding much more to his liking, signing up for a seven-year apprenticeship at Ditchburn and Mare (Chapter 3.1) in 1843/4 to learn the 'art and mystery' of iron shipbuilding.[6] He stayed with the shipyard through its various owners and incarnations until his death in 1907.[7]

A second contemporary document which survives is the historical catalogue which was produced to complement a showcase exhibition of the Thames Iron Works for the Festival of Empire, held at Crystal Palace, London, in 1911.[8] The 140-page catalogue is, along with the *TIWG*, another invaluable companion to any study of the Thames Iron Works and contains extensive listings of the ships, boats, engines and civil works constructed at the yard. A copy is held by the Science Museum at their archives in Wharton and is available for consultation on request.

Weights given for the ships discussed in this book are derived from several sources. Where possible, the weight has been defined according to the displacement tonnage of the ship. When derived from the historical catalogue[9] all weights are in displacement tons. Displacement tonnage describes the actual weight of the ship, reflected by the theoretical weight of water displaced by it. Displacement tons were recorded according to UK imperial measures with the ton equivalent to one long ton (2240lb or 1016kg or 1.016 metric tonnes). For some early naval ships, the known tonnage is given as the builder's measurement (abbreviated to bm) in tons. For ships built prior to *c* 1870 and not listed in the historical catalogue, it is not always clear from the sources whether displacement or builder's measurement tonnages are being used for vessels. It should also be noted that the historical catalogue gives the weights of ships at launch, and therefore often 'light'. Further fitting out or armouring would add further weight (Table 1).

Notes to Chapter 1

1 Arnold 2000, 5

2 Pollard 1950, 72

3 *Currency converter*

4 LAARC http://www.museumoflondon.org.uk/laarc

5 Murphy et al 1988, 163, quoted in Arnold 2000, 5

6 Lewis 1999, 113

7 Walker 2010, 139

8 SM, MS 616/1

9 Ibid

CHAPTER 2

19TH-CENTURY SHIPBUILDING ON THE THAMES

2.1 Wood and sail to iron and steam

The British Isles have always depended on navigation – around the coasts, along the rivers and canals, and to foreign lands. By the late 17th century a burgeoning merchant fleet operated alongside a newly reformed Royal Navy, greatly enlarged and modernised under the inspired guidance of Samuel Pepys.[1]

The port of London, with the many companies trading through it, generated the need for large numbers of ocean-going ships and also a myriad of vessels that were employed in facilitating trade on the river, such as barges and lighters. The trade also necessitated a huge amount of ship repair work which flourished on the Thames and survived long after the last of the shipbuilders had departed. By the middle of the 18th century, the Honourable East India Company alone required 12 new ships of the largest type annually, most of which were built by privately owned yards on the Thames between London Bridge, crossing the river between the City of London and Southwark, and Woolwich, in Greenwich (formerly Kent).[2] In 1790 imports through the port of London were 70% of the national total.[3]

The evolution of shipbuilding on the lower Thames in the 19th century can be broadly summarised as the transition from the building of comparatively small wooden sailing ships in a craft tradition at a large number of small private shipyards or the two naval dockyards at Woolwich and Deptford, Lewisham (formerly Kent), to the manufacture of much larger iron or steel-built, steam-powered ships by a few limited companies. These were organised on an industrial basis and often centred on a leading entrepreneur industrialist. Until the earlier part of the 19th century, the private shipbuilding companies were normally family run, the owners, shipwrights and related craftsmen passing on their skills and position to descendants who were apprenticed to the yard. Each shipbuilding region of the nation had its own peculiarities regarding boat design and craftsmanship – either the result of meeting local conditions and requirements, or simply out of the development in isolation of particular forms and techniques, with knowledge being passed down and developed by subsequent generations. Proximity to certain industries or institutions created the local market for different kinds of vessel. The existence of the Admiralty in London and the naval dockyards generated much warship

Table 1 Admiralty ships built at the Thames Iron Works and its predecessors, by year (based on Banbury 1971; and Thames Iron Works historical catalogue 1911 in SM, MS 616/1; latter references assumed to be tonnage at time of launch, before fitting out; tonnage calculated as builders' measurement (bm) and/or displacement (d)); the historical catalogue also lists warships built for the navies of Brazil, Denmark, Egypt, Greece, Japan, Peru, Prussia, Portugal, Romania, Russia, Spain and Turkey, as well as private foreign orders for vessels such as the Pope's own yacht, the *Immaculate Conception*, launched from the yard in 1859

Year laid down (where known)	Year launched	Name	Builder	Tonnage Banbury 1971	Tonnage SM, MS 616/1 (1911)	Details
-	1843	Princess Alice	Ditchburn and Mare	270bm	185d	paddle packet ship
?1843	1845	Trident	Ditchburn and Mare	850bm	798d	third-class iron paddle sloop
?1844	1845	Fairy	Ditchburn and Mare	312bm	210d	royal yacht
-	1845	Harpy	Ditchburn and Mare	344bm	415d	special service paddle ship
-	1845	Torch	Ditchburn and Mare	340bm	415d	iron paddle ?gun vessel
-	1845	Myrmidon	Ditchburn and Mare	374bm	415d	iron paddle ?gun vessel
-	1845/6	Onyx	Ditchburn and Mare	292bm	193d	iron paddle packet ship
-	1845/6	Violet	Ditchburn and Mare	292bm	193d	iron paddle packet ship
-	1846	Recruit	Ditchburn and Mare	462bm	462d	iron 12-gun sailing brig
-	1846	Antelope	C J Mare and Company	650bm	857d	iron paddle packet
-	1846	Sharpshooter	C J Mare and Company	503bm	585d	iron screw cargo
-	1846	Triton	C J Mare and Company	654bm	477d	iron paddle sloop
-	1847	Caradoc	C J Mare and Company	676bm	591d	cargo vessel
?1848	1849	Vulcan	C J Mare and Company	1747bm	2396d	iron screw frigate
1849/50	1851	Highflyer	C J Mare and Company	1153bm	1738d	wooden screw corvette
?1852	1853	Himalaya	C J Mare and Company	3428bm	3947d	troopship
-	1854	Urgent	C J Mare and Company	1981bm	2420d	despatch vessel
-	1854	Perseverance	C J Mare and Company	1967bm	2420d	despatch vessel
-	1854	Arrow	C J Mare and Company	477bm	-	despatch vessel
-	1854	Beagle	C J Mare and Company	477bm	-	despatch vessel
-	1854	Lynx	C J Mare and Company	477bm	-	despatch vessel
-	1854	Snake	C J Mare and Company	480bm	-	despatch vessel
-	1854	Industry	C J Mare and Company	638bm	998d	iron screw store ship
-	1854/5	Supply	C J Mare and Company	638bm	998d	iron screw store ship
-	1854/5	Transit	C J Mare and Company	2587bm	2775d	transport
-	1854/5	two mortar vessels	C J Mare and Company	-	-	mortar floats
-	1855	Meteor	C J Mare and Company	1469bm	-	floating battery
-	1855	Thunder	C J Mare and Company	1469bm	-	floating battery
-	1855	Nightingale	C J Mare and Company	232bm	-	gunboat (Albacore class)
-	1855/6	Alacrity	C J Mare and Company	675bm	605d	wooden screw gun vessel
-	1855/6	Vigilant	C J Mare and Company	680bm	605d	wooden screw gun vessel
-	1855/6	Bouncer	C J Mare and Company	232bm	-	gunboat (Albacore class)
-	1855/6	Hyaena	C J Mare and Company	232bm	-	gunboat (Albacore class)
-	1855/6	Violet	C J Mare and Company	232bm	-	gunboat (Albacore class)
-	1855/6	Wolf	C J Mare and Company	232bm	-	gunboat (Albacore class)
-	1855/6	Savage	C J Mare and Company	232bm	-	gunboat (Albacore class)
-	1856	Reynard	C J Mare and Company	682bm	605d	despatch boat
-	1856	Fox Hound	C J Mare and Company	681bm	605d	despatch boat
-	1856	20 HM mortar floats	Thames Iron Works	-	each 85d	mortar floats
1859	1860	Warrior	Thames Iron Works	9210d	8828d	armour-clad broadside
1861/2	1863	Minotaur	Thames Iron Works	10,690d	9870d	armour-clad broadside
1864	1866	Waterwitch	Thames Iron Works	1205d	1230d	armoured gunboat
1865	1866	Serapis	Thames Iron Works	6210d	6211d	torpedo boat
?1867	1869	Active	Thames Iron Works	3080d	3333d	iron screw corvette
?1867	1869	Volage	Thames Iron Works	3080d	3333d	iron screw corvette
1868	1870	Magdala	Thames Iron Works	3340d	3365d	coast defence
1870	1871	Cyclops	Thames Iron Works	3480d	3202d	coast defence
1872	1874	Rover	Thames Iron Works	3460d	3364d	iron screw corvette
?1873	1875	Superb	Thames Iron Works	9310d	8894d	armour-clad battery
1879	1880	Swift	Thames Iron Works	-	767d	composite gun vessel
1879	1880	Linnet	Thames Iron Works	756d	767d	composite gun vessel
?1881	?1881	?(Vilhena)	Thames Iron Works	-	144d	gunboat
1882	1885	Benbow	Thames Iron Works	10,600d	10,011d	barbette ship
1885	1887	Sans Pareil	Thames Iron Works	10,470d	10,538d	turret ship
1888	1890	Blenheim	Thames Iron Works	9000d	9039d	cruiser first class
1889/90	1892	Grafton	Thames Iron Works	7350d	7350d	cruiser first class
1889/90	1892	Theseus	Thames Iron Works	7350d	7350d	cruiser first class
1894	1895	Zebra	Thames Iron Works	340d	303d	torpedo boat destroyer
?1896	1896	British Ambassador's launch	Thames Iron Works	-	29d	launch vessel
1896	1898	Albion	Thames Iron Works	12,950d	12,950d	battleship first class
1899	1901	Duncan	Thames Iron Works	14,000d	14,000d	battleship first class
1899	1901	Cornwallis	Thames Iron Works	14,000d	14,000d	battleship first class
1902	1902	Sir Frederick Walker	Thames Iron Works	174d	174d	service launch
1902	1904	Black Prince	Thames Iron Works	13,550d	13,550d	cruiser first class
1908	1910	Nautilus	Thames Iron Works	915d	1060d	torpedo boat
1910	1911	Thunderer	Thames Iron Works	22,500d	22,500d	battleship

building work for the Thames shipyards. All the Admiralty ships built by the Thames Iron Works and its predecessors are shown in Table 1.

Over the course of the 19th century, the supremacy of the Thames as the nation's leading ship producer was to be challenged and ultimately defeated by a variety of factors. Warship production in the private shipyards of the Thames had declined by the early part of the century. The Napoleonic Wars did not provide the same upsurge of work for private shipbuilders as had the wars of the 18th century[4] and the drop-off in trade resulting from the political instability further affected the Thames shipyards. Their specialisation in, and eventual partial dependence on, the production of the East Indiamen (Fig 6) tied the Thames to the decline of their trade in the early part of the 19th century, with trade dwindling even before the ending of the Honourable East India Company's monopoly in 1813. While the Thames had focused on the East Indiamen, elsewhere in Britain massive strides had been made in the production of merchant vessels of different types. The north-east coast, for instance, had 'acquired a near monopoly of building colliers and whalers'.[5]
In the coming years, one of the most significant factors contributing to the decline of Thames private shipyards was the rise of the new material, iron.

Fig 6 Painting of the East Indiaman *Warley*, by Robert Salmon (1804); the ship was launched at Blackwall in 1796
(National Maritime Museum, Greenwich, London, BHC3707)

The use of iron as the main material for shipbuilding is inextricably linked with the developing technology of steam propulsion, firstly by paddle wheel and later by screw propeller. Innovations of propulsion inevitably led to larger ships with evolving structural requirements. Paradoxically, the potential of iron for the construction of ships of a hitherto unimaginable size itself necessitated engines of increasing power and fuel economy. The new technology was not developed in the old established shipyards, where wooden shipbuilding continued for the first few decades of the 19th century; thereafter these yards were either taken over by builders in iron or, due to their often small size or upriver location, they ceased activity altogether. Iron was the product of the industrial age. The early development of steam power with iron mostly took place in areas up to this time associated with heavy industry, rather than shipbuilding, and the innovators of the new technology were often those already well versed in the use of iron for civil engineering. Similarly, the progenitors of the new shipyards and their workforce were mostly drawn from industrial areas already employing iron and steam power. Boilermakers and iron foundry workers formed a large portion of those who travelled to work in the new shipyards.[6] The implications of this in terms of administrative organisation and working practices nationally were far reaching and will be discussed in Chapter 5.

The early steam vessels were generally still wooden-built ships, iron being used in some cases to provide strengthening. In London, the boats built in the 1820s and 30s for two of the main competing companies of the new passenger trade – the London and Gravesend and the London and Margate companies – were 'still rather primitive' with steam-engine power fitted to 'the hulls of old sailing ships'.[7] Where iron was used, it was almost always bought into the yards, prefabricated in iron foundries. Engines and machinery were also produced externally. The fitting of steam power to old sailing ship hulls or types brought with it several problems: the shapes of the hulls were not suited to powered propulsion; there was a constant risk of fire (wooden members sometimes became visibly charred in contact with hot metal); the structure was not rigid enough to cope with the forces exerted by the machinery; and often, especially in enclosed spaces, dry rot was caused by the steam. Screw propulsion, which gradually began to replace the paddle wheel, in particular exerted stresses and pressures on wooden-hulled boats that could cause structural issues and mechanical failures. In addition to these problems, wooden ships were limited in size by the nature and availability of the material.

Iron became an increasingly used component of ships as the technology of powered propulsion advanced, but there was a lag in time between the introduction of steam and the general application of iron to build the hulls of ships. Early iron-hulled vessels for the most part were built in the North, with iron canal boats operating on the Midlands Canal by 1813 and the *Vulcan*, a passenger barge built in 1819, on the Forth and Clyde Canal.[8] A major breakthrough came in 1822 with the first sea crossing of an iron-hulled boat, the 80hp *Aaron Manby*, from London to Le Havre (Seine-Maritime) and Paris, France (Fig 7). This was all the more surprising as the vessel was designed as a river boat.[9] The degree to which the new technology was being developed outside the old shipbuilding areas is shown by the fact that the *Aaron Manby* was created not in a shipyard, but in sections at the Horseley Iron Works in Staffordshire, from where it was sent to Rotherhithe (Surrey) to be assembled and launched in 1821. The vessel was the brainchild of Admiral Charles Napier, a man who relatively early realised the potential of iron shipbuilding and promoted its uptake by the navy. The vessel was in use primarily on the Loire (France) until 1855. The new iron building was mostly developed in the Midlands, the North and in Scotland, with increasing numbers of iron vessels launched by such names as David Napier, John Laird and William Fairbairn. Iron shipbuilding came late to the Thames, and again it was not a shipbuilder who can be credited with the launch but an industrialist. In 1831, the East India Company invited tenders for four iron steamboats and 'four accommodation vessels'.[10] One of these, the *Lord William Bentinck* was built by Maudslay, Field and Company of Lambeth and launched in 1832. It became the first of many iron ships to be launched on the Thames.

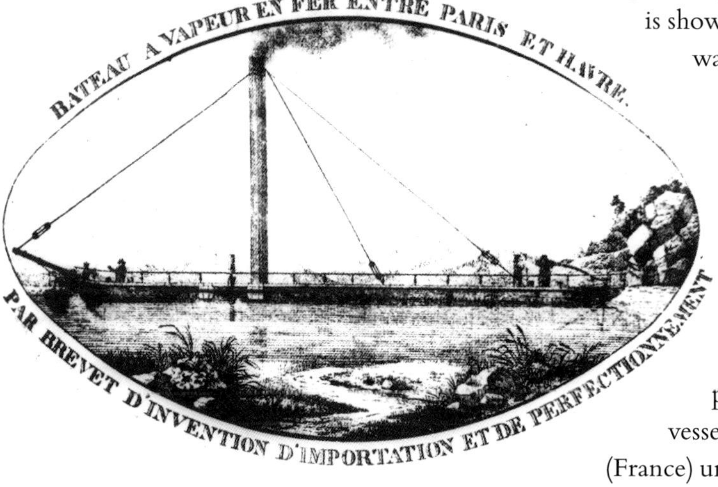

Fig 7 The *Aaron Manby*, launched in 1821; the French reads 'Iron steamship between Paris and Le Havre. Design protected by patents for its invention and improvement' (by permission of Sandwell Community History and Archives Service)

Steam-propelled boats had been produced on the Thames for a number of years and stoked the growth of industrial concerns on or near the Thames to develop and produce the ever larger and more efficient engines required. These works brought skills and techniques to marine engineering already learnt in terrestrial civil applications. Of the three largest and most significant builders of marine engines, John Penn and Sons of Greenwich, founded in 1799, were specialists in machinery for agricultural purposes and corn and flour mills. Maudslay, Field and Company (Maudslay, Sons and Field after 1833), founded in 1798 and taking premises in Lambeth in 1810, were specialists in precision machine tooling and machinery and proponents of standardisation. Rennie Brothers was formed in Southwark initially between 1821 and 1824. Brothers John and George were the sons of the famous civil engineer, John Rennie (the elder). With experience in both mechanical and civil engineering, the enterprise eventually extended to shipbuilding, with the building of a yard in Norman Road, Greenwich, which as J and G Rennie produced vessels from *c* 1833 onwards. Ultimately, J and G Rennie were the last of the significant shipbuilders to leave the Thames, outliving even Thames Iron Works – although in their final years of production in Greenwich, only relatively minor vessels were produced (Banbury lists vessels produced from 1859 to 1909 only[11]). In 1915 J and G Rennie moved to Wivenhoe (Essex) on the River Colne, where they survived as a business concern until 1930.[12]

The concentration of industrial expertise and the ready market for the new iron steam-powered ships led to the Thames taking a leading role in the boom of steamship building in the 1830s and 1840s. It was, however, really only during the 1840s that iron vessels began to be produced in any number, and as of 1850 iron construction tonnage only made up 9.5% of the United Kingdom's total output.[13] As a producer of both wooden and iron vessels, the Thames maintained its importance as a centre of shipbuilding, although other centres of iron shipbuilding, especially the Clyde, began to rival if not surpass the Thames over the next two decades. Mackrow places the decline on the Thames as beginning with the final departure of the old wooden shipbuilding firms such as Fletcher of Limehouse and Pitcher of Northfleet, which closed in 1861. With the final passing of the old wooden shipbuilding concerns, 'a great change came over the whole district, and the sawyers, caulkers, and shipwrights, etc., found their occupation all but gone'.[14]

The Admiralty was slower to furnish their fleets with steam-powered vessels than the merchant cargo or passenger operators. The naval dockyards maintained strongly traditional shipbuilding practices that operated according to established principles of craft and labour organisation. The yards and their working practices were suited to the building of wooden ships of great size and quality, but did not easily translate to the techniques and industrial organisation necessary for steam-powered and later, in particular, iron shipbuilding. The scale of the machinery shown in Fig 8 and produced in 1901 by the Thames Iron Works gives some idea of the changes that shipbuilding facilities had to undergo to accommodate the new technology.

Fig 8 Part of a steam engine for a merchant ship
(National Maritime Museum, Greenwich, London, H0465)

It is easy to paint a picture of the Admiralty as consisting entirely of recalcitrant traditionalists, but this was not the case and there existed those who promoted the adoption of technological innovation. They had first experimented with steam power with the *Comet* in 1822, which was followed by the Alban class paddle steam warship from 1824.[15] Progress was made over the next two decades with steam power although the ships remained primarily of wooden construction, with iron plates in the early 1840s still regarded as too easily damaged by enemy fire and less easily repaired. The success of the *Archimedes* in 1833, the world's first screw-propelled steam ship, engineered by Rennie, demonstrated the potential of this form of propulsion over paddle steamers. The screw was fairly readily taken up by commercial concerns and in 1843 HMS *Rattler*, the world's first screw-propelled warship, was launched. In trials in 1845 HMS *Rattler* outperformed the paddle ship HMS *Alecto*. During a nautical tug of war, HMS *Rattler* actually managed to pull HMS *Alecto*, paddles churning madly, backwards at a rate of 2½ knots (1 knot equals 1.852km per hour).[16]

The new Thames shipyards and large engineering concerns were ideally placed to meet the needs of the Admiralty in the development of their steam navy and early provision of iron-hulled boats. The first iron-hulled fighting ships ever acquired by the navy were HMS *Trident* and HMS *Recruit*, both built by Ditchburn and Mare (Chapter 3.1) and launched in 1845[17] and 1846[18] respectively.

Fig 9 Iron cased screw steam frigate HMS *Warrior*, 1861 (National Maritime Museum, Greenwich, London, PY9277)

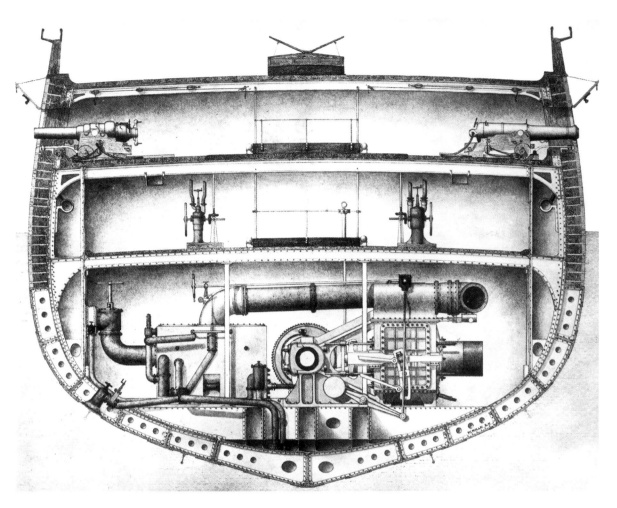

Fig 10 A cut-away view
of HMS *Warrior* (1860)
showing the internal
structure and two-
cylinder trunk steam
engine, made by John
Penn and Sons (*TIWG,*
no. 6, 1896, 45)
(Science Museum/Science &
Society Picture Library)

The degree to which the naval dockyards lagged behind the private shipyards
to which they contracted out much of the earlier work is evident in Mackrow's
account of the Admiralty visit to the Thames Iron Works during the
construction of HMS *Warrior* in 1859 or 1860 (Fig 9; Fig 10). 'I remember Mr
Warner, a weakly, consumptive man, English Government Inspector, saying:
"We have not come here, Mr Mackrow, *to teach*, we have come here *to learn*."
Up to this time the Admiralty only possessed a few iron sloops and transports,
mostly built by this firm'.[19] The Admiralty actually sent workers and managers
to the Thames Iron Works to learn the techniques necessary, such as the
longitudinal system of framing employed[20] to build the new iron battleship
HMS *Achilles*, launched at Chatham (Kent) in 1863.[21]

For a time at least the core of the new shipyards of the Thames would flourish
as builders of iron ships and it is during this period that London witnessed the
rise of the Thames Iron Works, arguably the greatest shipyard that the Thames
ever had.

2.2 Iron shipbuilding: raw materials and industrial processes

While both the naval dockyards and the private shipyards fabricated the vast majority of the component parts for the ships on their slips, raw materials such as timber, pitch and tar, and coal had to be bought into the yards from elsewhere. Partially created materials in unconverted form, such as bolts of canvas or iron bar, were also bought in. A good portion of the success or failure of a private yard lay in its ability to buy in these materials cheaply enough. The costs depended on transport distances and economies of scale, and thus the siting of a yard with respect to suppliers and transportation hubs was vital. Pollard states that the 'competitive advantage of British shipyards' viewed as a whole, was established in the period of 1860–80, when 'no other major country save America, whose resources were occupied elsewhere, had the iron, steel, and engineering capacity' for producing 'modern steamers on a large scale'.[22]

Much of the information for the internal industrial arrangements of the Thames Iron Works comes from Barry's 1863 reports on the dockyards and shipyards of the United Kingdom.[23] Barry criticised the myriad diversity of manufacture in the Royal Naval Dockyards in his damning report, pointing out that 'the Admiralty in addition to constructing and repairing ships, follow no fewer than fifty industrial pursuits'.[24] He was an outspoken advocate of private enterprise and believed strongly in the subcontracting out of work by shipbuilders to specialists as required. He clearly considered the dockyards to be backwards places, with their atavism the result of a failure 'to adapt the manufactures of the dockyards to the ever-changing circumstances of the country'.[25] While there was clearly a lot of underuse, this was perhaps unfair criticism as the purpose of the dockyards was to have enough capacity to cope with the sudden demands brought on by an international crisis or war.

Barry contrasted the supposed idleness and waste of the Royal Naval Dockyards with the model of the private shipyard whose 'rule is the golden one, of investing capital in the direction and to the extent that it is really profitable'.[26] He continued 'The Thames Iron Shipbuilding Company, and other large engineering firms, have their engineer shops, their saw mills, their brass foundries, &c.; but these are mere conveniences, and all subordinate to the great purpose of … building ships'.[27] The 'colossal scale' of the largest private shipbuilding enterprises allowed this level of industrial specialisation to be profitable, although in times of slack the maintenance of such large and diverse enterprises could be ruinous. Only two shipyards on the Thames ever produced their own iron, the Thames Iron Works and the Millwall Iron Works, and both of these were the result of the vision of Charles Mare, the co-founder of Ditchburn and Mare (Chapter 3). Recognising the benefits of large economies of scale and the ready and cheap supply of iron in the form of scrap, Mare based his yards around the idea of vertical integration (Chapter 3.2), whereby the conversion of materials to components would be undertaken on site, so long as the costs of doing so were cheaper than buying in. The Thames Iron Works increased its iron-making capacity beyond even that of its own yard, purchasing the Phoenix Iron Works, Millwall, around 1862/3.[28] The 1850s and 1860s were, however, the heyday of iron production in the yards, as after the 1860s, the drop-off in demand, and also changes in the technology of iron and steel production, began to make the production of wrought iron from scrap in great quantities unnecessary and unprofitable. Indeed, increased stringency from Lloyd's regarding their classification of vessels (the benchmark rating of a ship's quality) had been introduced in 1855, reducing the amount of scrap that could be included in high-grade metal, and pointing to the end for the viability of any vertically integrated model including iron production (from scrap) for ships in London.[29]

Coal

The siting of the Thames Iron Works played a large part in its initial and continuing success, with access to raw materials provided by rail and by the wharfs fronting the Thames a short distance away (Fig 27). The creation of the Victoria Dock (later Royal Victoria Dock, from 1880)[30] brought further cost savings to the developing heavy industries on the Lea, which by the mid 1850s had largely replaced the earlier tidal mills with 'the abundant but polluting energy of seaborne coal'.[31]

The Thames Iron Works required huge quantities of coal so its cost had obvious implications. It is not entirely clear where the ironworks got this coal from. The works had access to its own siding (Fig 27) of the Great Eastern Railway (earlier the Eastern Counties Railway) from which materials could be transferred to an extensive tramline system which 'ramifies through the works'.[32] The coal appears to have been brought into the yard from this siding. The plant on the tramways for hauling materials around developed over the life of the yard, from manhandled trollies in the early life of the yard to steam-powered locomotive cranes during the final years.

In the mid 19th century, seaborne coal was much cheaper than that transported by land and the opening of Cory and Son, coal importers, in the mid 1850s just south-west of Victoria Dock and within a stone's throw of the ironworks further reduced the price of coal to 7s 6d per ton. Railway-supplied coal at the time cost 12s 6d.[33] The ironworks clearly had a relationship with Cory and Sons, selling them a floating river wharf 'Atlas' in 1859; this had originally been intended for a company set on raising shipwrecks but which failed. The floating wharf further reduced the price of coal by negating dock fees.

Given the potential savings of importing the coal through Cory and Sons, it seems strange then that the Thames Iron Works appears to have 'gotten its coals used at the works, amounting to about 50000 tons [50,800 tonnes] per annum … by rail direct from the pit's mouth in Yorkshire'.[34] This is backed up by a description of the works by Miall who visited the works in 1893. When Miall's companion asked if the works burnt 'Best Welsh', the 'fireman … replied with a grin, that they only burnt "Common Yorkshire"'.[35] Bituminous coal, of which the south Yorkshire coalfield was in plentiful supply,[36] was known to provide the best fuel for reverbatory-type furnaces. The ironworks may have employed a single source best suited to their needs. If the coal was delivered direct by rail from this source, perhaps the Thames Iron Works were able to undercut the costs of bringing it by sea.

Timber

Timber was employed in vast quantities in the yard (Fig 11). While there are obvious uses for timber during the age of the wooden-built ships, it may come as a surprise that the Thames Iron Works consumed such quantities. Timber was employed for several purposes at the yard. Firstly, it served as the material from which the slipways were constructed and also the hundreds of piles on which the buildings and the slipways were built. The pine (*Pinus* sp) for this purpose probably came from either the Baltic or from Canada.

The vast majority of timber used at the yard was imported from the colonies or elsewhere in the world where shipbuilding and industry had not completely denuded the land of suitable trees. 'The havoc wrought upon the oak forests of Britain' out of which many of the famous British warships of the previous two centuries had been built, meant that from the turn of the 19th century, a suitable replacement had to be found.[37] Subsequent trials with

Fig 11 The timber yard at the Thames Iron Works showing timber stacked at the rear of the sawmills in 1894; the timber consists of '1300 loads waiting to be cut up into deck planks and backing for the armour-plates of the new battleship Fuji' (*Engineer* 1895, 571 fig 6) (Graces Guides)

various woods showed that teak (*Tectona grandis* sp) both replicated the strength and durability of oak (*Quercus* sp), while being resistant to the 'galvanic action' of being placed with iron in the water. The composite ships in the mid 1850s that used oak, found that tannins in the wood reacted with the metal and this 'galvanic action' caused the destruction of the metal parts. The suitability of teak, and the capacity of the new large steamers to convey it half the way round the world, led to its uptake by navies and shipbuilders on an industrial scale – although it had already been used by those countries it was being imported from for centuries. In India, the *TIWG* says in 1901,[38] the forests had 'long been almost exhausted' and teak was sought in 'Siam [modern-day Thailand] and Burma [modern-day Myanmar]', south-east Asia (Fig 12).

Fig 12 Elephants were employed in their thousands in the teak trade, working with mahouts to move vast quantities of timber from the jungles of 'Siam and Burma' to rivers along which the timber could be brought to port
(Barking and Dagenham Archives and Local Studies Centre, 623.82)

Teak formed the backing for the armour plating of HMS *Warrior* and other ironclad ships. It was also used as decking for ships, although the decking of HMS *Warrior* itself was of Dantzig oak (exported through the port of Dantzig, now in Poland).[39] Teak continued to be utilised in ships for the Admiralty and foreign powers also, with the *TIWG* describing teak as 'the king of all shipbuilding woods' found.[40]

Timber also continued to be used at the yard for boatbuilding. Wooden vessels, albeit sometimes plated with iron, were produced on the Middlesex side of the yard until the early 1860s, whereafter the timber yards and sawmills moved over to the Essex bank. From 1895 the yard undertook to build large numbers of wooden vessels for the Royal National Lifeboat Institution (RNLI) and other bodies (Chapter 3.3).

How iron was made

The iron produced at the Thames Iron Works was wrought iron. Between the 1840s and 1860s, before steel manufacture improved, wrought iron was the best material available for shipbuilding, being far less brittle than either cast iron or mild steel. The low carbon content and retention of a quantity of slag (stringers) within the wrought iron also helped to give it a fibrous consistency.

The wrought (literally 'worked') iron made at the works was derived mostly from scrap. It was commented in *Mechanics' Magazine* in 1861[41] that earlier in the life of the yard, a ratio of one part puddled iron to three parts scrap had been used (presumably during the tenure of C J Mare: Chapter 3.2), but that this had been discontinued, with all iron produced certainly by 1861 being derived from scrap of differing qualities. The puddled iron would have been made in reverbatory, specifically puddling, furnaces several of which the yard possessed (Fig 13).

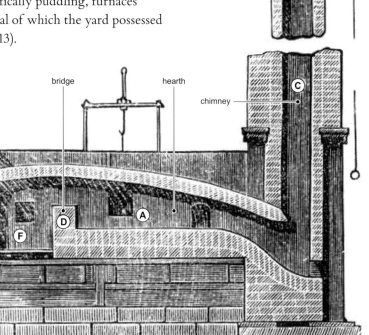

Fig 13 Schematic drawing of a typical puddling furnace (after Hartshorne 1881, 609 fig 15.4): A, the hearth; C, the chimney with a damper at the summit to regulate the draught; D, a bridge separating the grate from the hearth, preventing the direct contact of the fuel with the iron; and F, the grate or fireplace

The puddling process had been invented and patented by Henry Cort by 1784.[42] It involved stirring or working molten pig iron in an oxidising atmosphere to remove the carbon from it.[43] The process was further refined by Joseph Hall at Tipton (Staffordshire) in the early 19th century, who invented wet puddling, which added scrap to the charge, and later iron oxide (rust). This caused the molten charge to boil violently as it released carbon dioxide bubbles. Hall also introduced the practice of using roasted tap cinder (slag from the previous furnace firings) to line the floor of the hearth, massively reducing the amount of iron lost compared with the previous sand bedding.[44]

The puddling furnace was an improvement on previous smelting techniques, and allowed for far greater quantities of iron to be produced. The process did not require the use of charcoal and the fuel source for the firing was kept separate from the material being transformed, with only the gases and heat from the firing coming into contact with the pooling iron. The result was a malleable material that could be worked by pressure into the diverse forms of sufficient strength required for iron ships. The process was a very dirty and exhausting one, subjecting the workers to extremes of heat and fumes, and it is unsurprising that the 'puddlers' had a reduced life expectancy because of it, with many dying in their 30s.[45]

The scrap brought into the yard was a truly 'miscellaneous assortment … old horse-shoes and clog-irons, bucket handles, tea trays, snuffers, old door locks and hinges, tailors' scissors, scythes, and boat hooks'.[46] The article in *Mechanics' Magazine* goes on to describe the process by which the scrap was given new life, 'Old "Edax Rerum",[47] in the shape of a huge shearing machine, chews them into convenient sizes for faggoting with as much indifference as if they were so many carrots or lettuces'.[48] The pieces of broken up scrap were then made into little heaps 'between two deal boards, about a foot and a-half square [0.14m²], the larger pieces of boiler-plate and chopped wheel tires forming the outside, while the interior is filled up with small odds and ends'.[49] This work was mostly undertaken by women.

Barry describes how these little heaps of 'horseshoes, nails, tongs, pokers and scrap iron' were then placed in a furnace to be 'baked' into iron 'blooms'.[50] The *Mechanics' Magazine* article relates that the metal would be removed when the mass of scrap had reached 'a state of incipient fusion' and that the mass would be subjected to a tilt hammer to 'beat out the slag and fused dross, and consolidate it into a compact mass'.[51] The resultant lump was reheated in a furnace to soften it and then rolled into a slab about 6in (152.4mm) breadth and ¾in (19.05mm) thick. The slabs were then cut up again into short lengths for faggoting, and the process of baking and rolling would be repeated, though this time with the inclusion of broken up locomotive wheel tires if they were being used. These were '£2 to £3 per ton more expensive than the scrap' for the yard to buy in,[52] though added much strength to the resultant iron produced. The final product would likely be reheated and rolled again at least one more time, though often multiple times, in order to ensure consistency throughout the material. The large slabs formed were about 5cwt (254kg) each. They would then be taken to be reheated in further furnaces near the steam hammers, which could combine the slabs into plates weighing from between 3 and 4 tons (3.05–4.06 tonnes).[53] At the time of writing in 1861, the *Mechanics' Magazine* article claimed there were 'no less than six-steam hammers, and two rolling mills' employed.[54]

The Bessemer process, developed in the mid 1850s and refined over the next few years, led for the first time to the production of strong steel in large quantities and displaced the puddling furnace altogether after the mid 1860s. The forging of armour plate and the creation of crank shafts had been very profitable work for the ironworks. However, following the introduction of Joseph Whitworth's compressed steel and later the malleable cast steel, the yard could no longer prosper using the abundant local scrap. Miall describes casting at the yard using a new type of steel 'patented by … a Mr Radcliffe'.[55] He describes the heating of 'ore' for the steel in furnaces, so unless he was mistaken, it does seem as if at least some steel production was going on at the yard at the time. Writing in September of 1897, however, Mackrow lamented the departure of Mr Hardy, who had been the manager of the rolling mills since the company's inception and was leaving 'as he was only idling, no work for the mills coming in'.[56]

The use of steam hammers

The steam hammers at the yard were of the type developed by James Nasmyth, the first working model having been built by him in 1842 (Fig 14).[57] The steam hammer was necessitated by the increasingly large shafts and cranks required for locomotives and steamers. They operated on the fairly simple principle of the raising of a heavy hammer by steam pressure, which was allowed to drop under gravity to strike a piece of metal on an anvil. The metal would be manipulated to shape it under the repeated blows. Later, double action steam hammers increased the force of the blow by accelerating the drop with steam pressure. Other improvements and replacements were made to the steam hammers utilised at the ironworks as newer technology became available, such as the superseding of Nasmyth's original complex gearing by a much simpler lever and rod mechanism.[58] A description of a steam hammer at the Thames Iron Works is given by Miall, who visited the works in 1893 where he saw being drawn out of a furnace 'a lump of iron, weighing several hundredweight, and raised to such an intense heat that, as it was swung round to where the hammer was placed, drops of liquid metal ran from its glowing mass, and blue flames flickered round its sides'.[59] He then observed 'the huge steam hammer, 120 tons [121.9 tonnes] in weight, rained down blows that shook the ground beneath our feet, there flew off from the soft iron showers of brilliant sparks'.[60] The metal was quickly turned under the blows 'with a wonderful adroitness … so that in a couple of minutes, or even less, it had been knocked into the shape required'.[61] Miall also mentioned that the force of the blows flattened the anvils, 'blocks of iron weighing several tons', beyond use within a fairly short time necessitating their replacement.[62]

The steam hammers at the works were responsible for turning out its armour plate, with those for HMS *Warrior* being made in this way from scrap railway carriage wheels, and production of armour plate continuing at least through the 1860s. The old scrap wrought iron was not deemed strong enough for the purposes of armour plating after the late 1870s, although the steam hammers would still have been used for producing heavy forgings such as crank shafts.

Fig 14 A steam hammer of the type designed by Nasmyth and employed at the ironworks
(Science Museum/Science & Society Picture Library)

The steam hammers seem to have largely gone out of use at the works not long after the visit by Miall; by 1895 the 'complete plant for making bar and plate iron and heavy forgings … [were] disused, the ground and buildings being gradually appropriated for other purposes'.[63] These disused areas no doubt refer in part to puddling furnaces and steam hammers. The hydraulic press, of which the yard was by then in possession,[64] took over some of the work. The ironworks may have been producing components from steel in significant quantities at least until the end of the 19th century; however, the cost implications of no longer being able to use the readily available scrap to make their own metal would clearly have been a great disadvantage to the yard.

The production of armour plating and the advent of steel

John Samuda Benthall, writing in the *TIWG* gives us a short history of armour plating.[65] The first armour plates for a warship were rolled in 1855 by Park Gate Steel and Iron Company in south Yorkshire for the *Terror*.[66] Armour plating could either be rolled or steam hammered, with arguments for both made, although there was little difference between them in strength in the early years of armour plating. Rapid development in manufacturing took place after 1859, with the building of the ironclad fleet, with plates increasing in thickness, although 'the material remained the same until 1876',[67] when the first trial took place at Spezzia (Italy) of a solid steel plate created by a French company, Messrs Schneider of Creusot. Subsequent trials in the United Kingdom resulted in the compound plate of steel over wrought iron backing, first employed by Samuda Brothers on the Argentine warship *Almirante Brown* and then for the Admiralty on HMS *Ajax* in 1880. In the early 1860s, armour – such as on HMS *Warrior* – had been wrought iron over timber backing, normally teak (*Tectona grandis* sp).[68]

Solid steel plates were made in France and elsewhere, but were not taken up by the Admiralty until the development *c* 1889 of solid steel plates by Vickers, Sons and Co.[69] In the early 1890s, American engineer Hayward Augustus Harvey invented a process for using nickel steel to make armour plate, using cementation and chilling by cold spray. The process was taken up and improved by Vickers and Sons, and their 'Harveyed steel' armour plate became the benchmark for the Admiralty at home and for other maritime nations abroad. The Japanese ship *Fuji*, built at the Thames Iron Works and launched in 1896, employed 'Harveyed steel' armour.[70]

Benthall, working at the Vickers works in Sheffield (Yorkshire, West Riding), described how once the size and shape of plates had been worked out, ingots were ordered.[71] In the transformation of the steel into the armour plate, 'The mixture of steel and the charging into the furnaces is all arranged for, and when the steel is at its proper heat it is run into buckets, and from thence it is taken to the mould awaiting it in the casting pit. Here it is cast into the ingot and becomes the first stage of an armour plate'.[72] The plates undergo further stages, going to the forging shop to be heated and hydraulically pressed into a slab. The slab was transferred to the rolling mills, then to the machine shop for cutting, then to the carburising furnaces where it would stay for a fortnight or so. From here it would be heated again and bent under hydraulic press to shape, before being further machined to shape following testing. Then it would be sent to a hardening plant where the plate would be heated and then cooled by jets of water until cold. It would then return to the machine shop for inspection and to be checked before making its final journey via railway to the 'ship it is destined to protect'.[73]

It is not clear how long Thames Iron Works made armour plate. It is likely that they lacked the capacity to keep up with the development at Vickers and certainly by the time of the *Fuji*, whose armour plate was produced at Vickers,[74] armour plate was produced elsewhere and then bought into the yard. It seems the ironworks may have had some involvement in production as late as 1893, although to what extent is not clear. Miall described 'new machinery for preparing armour plates … by passing them under rollers at high pressure – a process which, up to the present, has not been performed on the premises'.[75] Whether the Thames Iron Works was creating the armour plates or merely finishing them is not told. Miall maybe mistook normal ship plating for armour plate.

Riveting

Ships today are generally welded together, with the various sections, often weighing hundreds of tons, prefabricated and then taken to the launch site to be joined together. Prior to the 1940s, however, ships were built by a different process. The iron or steel bars and angles for the structure and the plates were cut, shaped and bent as required in the workshops of the yard and the required rivet holes punched or drilled.[76] These piecemeal components were then assembled at the slip and riveted together. The job of riveting up frames and plates was one of the most labour intensive, dangerous and exhausting in the yard.

Whereas the Thames Iron Works generally utilised up to date machinery, all the riveting was carried out by hand until the early 1890s when it began to be replaced by mechanical means. Mackrow wrote in 1895 'the system of riveting up frames by hydraulic riveters instead of by hand has greatly reduced the cost of this work, at the same time facilitating the erection of the ship'.[77] That is not to say that all manual riveting was phased out, as there were situations where machinery could not be applied and certainly the plating of the hull was still carried out by hand right up until the closure of the yard. Machinery notwithstanding, during the creation of a ship or a civil structure, teams of riveters would make up a good portion of the workforce at the works. In tribute to the thousands of men and boys, without whose millions of rivets the structure of the British Empire would never have existed, there follows a description of the riveting process.

The process changed little over the second half of the 19th century, with accounts of riveting work from the 1860s[78] describing the same methods as those employed on the *Titanic* from 1909 to 1911.[79] The riveters formed close-knit teams of four or five. Each team generally consisted of one or two riveters or 'bashers', a 'holder on' or 'holder up', a 'heater boy' (not necessarily a boy but traditionally called so) and a 'catch boy' or 'putter in'. The rivets were, in their most basic form, a short, stubby length of iron or steel with a head like a tack and a point. They varied in size depending on such factors as the thickness of the hull plates they were joining and corresponded to the pre-prepared holes they were to fill. The rivet would be heated until red hot and the entire operation undertaken needed to secure the rivet before it cooled down.

The heater boy would generally use a brazier or 'portable hearth'[80] set up as close to the riveting work as possible to heat the rivets. The rivets might be heated in 'shallow pans over coals'[81] or arranged in an iron plate that held the points in the fire[82] and protected the heads from direct contact with the coals (Fig 15). Sometimes the rivets were simply placed directly into the fire. The fire was blasted by hand- or foot-operated bellows worked by the heater boy until the rivets glowed red. In some instances, where large ships were being built, the rivet hearths were connected to a blowing engine instead of a bellows; however, this could only occur if the ships were near enough to machine sheds to allow it.[83] The heated rivets would then either be passed with long tongs[84] or thrown to the catch boy, who caught the rivet in a wooden bucket.[85]

The catch boy then placed the rivet into the hole with tongs[86] or passed it to the holder up to do so. Sometimes the holder up would also take on the role of catch boy.[87] The holder up would drive the rivet in with his hammer which weighed between 10lb and 40lb (4.54–18.14kg)[88] and then hold their hammer or a 'dolly' (a short bar of iron 10–30lb or 4.54–13.61kg in weight) over the head of the rivet. Working on the other side of the plate, the riveters[89] would strike several blows around the rivet to bring the plates together (Fig 15), and then beat the point with their 2–7lb (0.91–3.18kg) hammer (a specialised mallet with a slender, elongated head; Fig 16),[90] squashing the rivet to fill the hole and shaping the rivet point. This was all done at speed so that the 'clenching-over' could

Fig 15 Fragment of iron plate <20> with diagram showing <20> as part of a butt-strap used to rivet two plates together (after Reed 1869, 205 fig 149) (scale, photograph, c 1:4)

<20>

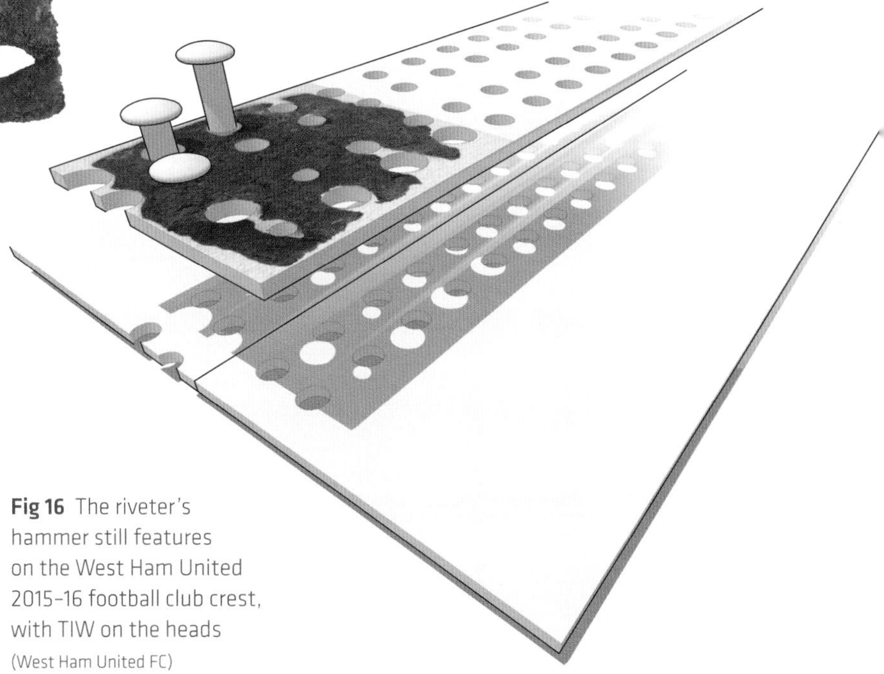

Fig 16 The riveter's hammer still features on the West Ham United 2015-16 football club crest, with TIW on the heads (West Ham United FC)

THE THAMES IRON WORKS 1837–1912

be completed before the red-hot rivet cooled.[91] The cooling of the rivet would then further draw the two plates together as the rivet contracted.

Riveters were generally paid by the number of rivets they completed, so while the work was available the teams of men worked as hard and for as long as possible each day. The work was undertaken at height, with no security for the workers who had to brave both the elements and the dangers of falling, not to mention the red-hot rivets and sparks of flashing metal or the heavy hammers themselves. Woe to the catch boy who dropped a red-hot rivet from several stories up. The teams were fiercely competitive and record books were meticulously kept by the yards for each of the teams' outputs. The record for a four-man riveting team at Belfast's (County Antrim) Harland and Wolff firm which built the *Titanic* was 'over 12,000 rivets driven in a single six-day week in the summer of 1909'.[92] That a group of men could perform the arduous and exhausting task, rivet after red-hot rivet, 2000 times over the course of a long summer's day and then repeat it day after day is an amazing feat of human endurance.

Notes to Chapter 2

1 Miles 1841, 23–6
2 Banbury 1971, 42
3 Arnold 2000, 9
4 Ibid, 7
5 Banbury 1971, 44
6 Ibid, 60
7 Arnold 2000, 13–14
8 Ibid, 10
9 Byrne 1864, 167
10 Smith 1924, quoted in Arnold 2000, 11
11 Banbury 1971, 238–41
12 Ibid, 230
13 Slaven 1980, 113, cited in Arnold 2000, 15
14 G Mackrow in *TIWG*, no. 3, 1895, 75
15 Evans 2004, 9
16 *HMS* Rattler
17 *ILN*, 27 December 1845, 404
18 *Ships list* a
19 *TIWG*, no. 1, 1895, 4
20 Bowen 1945, 375
21 Evans 2004, 163
22 Pollard 1957, 444

23 Barry 1863a; 1863b
24 Barry 1863b, 15
25 Ibid, 16
26 Ibid, 20
27 Ibid, 21
28 Ibid, 67
29 Pollard 1950, 76
30 *Royal Victoria Dock*
31 Clifford 2012, 45
32 *Engineer* 1894, 568
33 Crouch 1900, 64, quoted in Clifford 2012, 41
34 *ILN*, 6 October 1866, 348
35 Miall 1893, 172
36 Hill 2001, 20
37 *TIWG*, no. 28, 1901, 151
38 Ibid
39 Wells 1987, 42
40 *TIWG*, no. 28, 1901, 151
41 *Mechanics' Mag* 1861, 95
42 Dodd 1858b, 5
43 Byrne 1864, 21
44 Landes 1969, 33
45 Ibid, 218
46 *Mechanics' Mag* 1861, 95

47 Edax Rerum: Latin 'the devourer of all things' as in *tempus edax rerum* – 'time, the devourer of all things'.
48 *Mechanics' Mag* 1861, 95
49 Ibid
50 Barry 1863b, 65
51 *Mechanics' Mag* 1861, 95
52 Ibid
53 Ibid
54 Ibid
55 Miall 1893, 176
56 *TIWG*, no. 12, 1897, 154
57 Nasmyth and Smiles 1883, 248–9
58 *Mechanics' Mag* 1861, 95
59 Miall 1893, 176
60 Ibid
61 Ibid
62 Ibid
63 *Engineer* 1894, 567
64 SM, MS 616/1, 95
65 *TIWG*, nos 2 and 3, 1895
66 *TIWG*, no. 2, 1895, 52
67 Ibid

68 Wells 1987, 42
69 *TIWG*, no. 2, 1895, 53
70 SM, MS 616/1, 7
71 *TIWG*, no. 3, 1895, 91
72 Ibid
73 Ibid, 92
74 *TIWG*, no. 5, 1896, 12
75 Miall 1893, 176
76 *John Readhead's shipyard*
77 *TIWG*, no. 1, 1895, 6
78 Reed 1869, 340
79 *The lads in the shipyard*
80 Reed 1869, 340
81 Belton 2010, 10
82 Reed 1869, 340
83 Ibid
84 Belton 2010, 10
85 *The lads in the shipyard*
86 Ibid
87 Reed 1869, 340
88 Ibid, 341
89 *The lads in the shipyard*
90 Belton 2010, 10
91 *John Readhead's shipyard*
92 *The lads in the shipyard*

CHAPTER 3

A HISTORY OF THE THAMES IRON WORKS

3.1 Ditchburn and Mare (1837–47)

The enterprise which was later to become the Thames Iron Works and Shipbuilding Company began its life as the Ditchburn and Mare Shipbuilding Company, the first shipyard dedicated to building iron ships on the Thames. It was founded in 1837 by the shipwright Thomas Ditchburn and the industrial entrepreneur Charles Mare.

Thomas Joseph Ditchburn (1799–1870)

Thomas Ditchburn (Fig 17), a somewhat overlooked figure in the development of iron shipbuilding, contributed greatly to the transition from wooden sailing vessels to iron, steam-powered ones. Born in Chatham on 14 December 1799,[1] the son of shipwright Henry Ditchburn, he was apprenticed at the Royal Naval Dockyard then aged about 11. He worked hard and learnt quickly, eventually coming to the attention of Sir Robert Seppings, surveyor to the navy. It was reckoned at the end of his apprenticeship that in seven years he had been absent for a total of only one day.[2] At some time between 1822 and 1824,[3] though still very young, he became superintendent at the wooden shipbuilders Fletcher, Son and Fearnhall of Limehouse, where he remained until 1837.[4] Under his stewardship the firm developed a reputation for fast steam vessels, particularly paddle steamers for the burgeoning passenger trade. The demand for fast steamers was very great, with a plethora of newly formed companies competing on routes such as London to Margate (Kent). At its peak the Thames shipyards were supplying an industry that had an annual turnover of over a million excursionists and holidaymakers (activities made newly available to the masses) to the Kent coast alone.[5]

Fig 17 Portrait of Thomas J Ditchburn (*TIWG*, no. 15, 1898, 116) (National Maritime Museum, Greenwich, London, 629.12)

Ditchburn was an innovative thinker and observed that the traditional shapes of vessels, though evolved over centuries to suit the manifold applications of sail, did not suit power by steam. Mackrow, in the *TIWG* relates that *c* 1830, Ditchburn had produced a steamer for one of these companies – the *Royal George* – which consistently beat the fastest boat of its rivals – the *Magnet*.[6] He was asked to alter the *Magnet*, adjusting its bows so it became itself one of the fastest boats plying the trade. The *Magnet* so impressed that Fletcher, Son and Fearnhall became a prodigious producer of fast vessels and built or altered 'some of the most celebrated boats of the day'.[7] Ditchburn helped to lay the design foundations for the new steam-propelled boats, although he was certainly not the sole observer of the need to alter the shapes of the new ships. The Scottish engineer John Scott Russell (1808–82) conducted over 20,000 experiments[8] starting in 1834[9] which led to the development of his wave principle for ships.[10] The bows of vessels, previously rounded ('cod's head')[11] to accommodate the maximum amount of cargo, began to be altered towards a convex 'versine' form which dramatically reduced resistance to a ship's forward movement. Ditchburn became convinced that iron was the future of shipbuilding and, much to the horror of his wooden shipbuilding contemporaries, some of whom literally thought that Ditchburn was out of his mind, he struck out on his own in partnership with the young and ambitious Charles Mare in 1837 in Deptford. The same year he married Helen Kenney (1805–91) in Stepney, Tower Hamlets (formerly Middlesex),[12] and after the business moved to Blackwall in 1838 he lived in Palm Cottage on East India Dock Road with his wife and children.[13]

Charles John Mare (*c* 1814–98)

Charles John Mare was neither from London, nor from a shipbuilding background (Fig 18). Banbury charmingly describes Mare as having 'a passion for shipbuilding which misfortune never quenched' and notes his birthplace as 'Derbyshire, which is a long way from the sea'.[14] Baptism records seem to suggest that Mare was not from Derbyshire (though he may have been born there), but near Newcastle under Lyme in Staffordshire, also a long way from the sea.[15] His family moved to Cheshire when he was young and he was raised there in the family house 'Broomlands' at Hatherton.[16]

In 1832, he was articled with a firm in Doctors' Commons in the City of London to be trained as a solicitor.[17] Mare was evidently expected to pursue this course and perhaps return to a respectable provincial life (he took over the titles of Lord of the Manor of Hatherton and Shavington-cum-Gristy on his father's death in 1841), but instead he announced his intention to pursue a career as a shipbuilder and entered into partnership with Ditchburn in 1837. Mackrow's obituary of Mare states that he subsequently leased the family home and ploughed the proceeds into his shipbuilding business, though it is not clear when this occurred.[18]

This propensity for risk-taking and impulsive wilfulness marked the life of Mare and much of his success, and ultimately his failure, can perhaps be

Fig 18 Portrait of Charles J Mare (*TIWG*, no. 15, 1898, 117) (National Maritime Museum, Greenwich, London, 629.12)

attributed to it. It is not clear how the partnership that resulted in Ditchburn and Mare came to be. The lack of an establishment in this entirely new industry enabled many young men to rise to prominence and fortune quickly, but Mare's case was extreme – forming a partnership at only 22 or 23 years of age and seemingly without any experience in shipbuilding whatsoever. Ditchburn, being the taciturn and older man, and himself having experienced responsibility from a young age, may have been a steadying influence on Mare and certainly brought to the partnership the full breath of his shipbuilding talent and reputation. Mare seems to have brought to the business a boundless enthusiasm and dynamism. Mackrow, who joined the yard in 1843 or 1844 as a boy, describes him as 'a gentleman of strong will, and if he set his mind upon a project he would carry it out'.[19]

On 21 December 1843, Charles Mare married Mary Rolt, the daughter of the prominent Greenwich MP, Peter Rolt.[20] This connection brought a wealth of contacts and influence to the fledgling shipyard as Rolt was a well-known timber merchant[21] and his family had a background in shipbuilding.[22] Peter Rolt's father-in-law, Thomas Brocklebank, was one of the founders of the General Steam Navigation Company,[23] which brought work to C J Mare and Company (below, 3.2) and helped them, along with orders from Peninsula and Oriental Steam Navigation Company and the General Screw Steam Shipping Company, to become one of the prominent yards producing steamers at the time.[24] Writing in 1854, the *London Illustrated News* (*ILN*) was taken to remark that the output of C J Mare and Company (presumably including Ditchburn and Mare) had almost exceeded 400 vessels.[25] This is probably a slight overestimate, being based on the individual order numbers in the yard accounts (A1-100, B1-100 and so on), as some of these orders were not built. However, Mackrow writes that by the end of C J Mare's time as a shipbuilder, D.54 had been completed, implying 354 orders had been placed, many of which were built.[26]

Charles Mare was known for his largesse and acts of generosity, and for spending money generally. He raced horses at Newmarket (Suffolk/Cambridgeshire) and expended great sums on estates in Cheshire, Newmarket and Staffordshire. He also had extensive investments outside of the Thames Iron Works though it seems that his gambles did not always pay off. He ultimately lost £38,000 worth of shares in the General Steam Navigation Company and also spent £16,000 on becoming Member of Parliament for Plymouth, Devon (a position he briefly held from 1852 until his election was declared void on petition) and running the *Plymouth Mail* newspaper.[27] The Mare family certainly did not live frugally, and their lavish lifestyle brought with it social advancement. Mary Mare was presented at Court and became a favourite of Queen Victoria, while Charles was good friends with Benjamin Disraeli.[28]

The shipyard

Ditchburn and Mare was originally located at Deptford but, after a fire destroyed their yard, the firm relocated to Blackwall where, in 1838, they took over the premises of the bankrupt shipbuilders, William and Benjamin Wallis.[29] The new yard was at Orchard Place, on the west (Middlesex) bank of the River Lea at Bow Creek (Fig 19). It was well situated in an area not far to the east of the East India Docks and near to the venerable old shipbuilding establishment, the Blackwall Yard.[30] At the time of foundation, the locality was still not totally developed. The Orchard House inn, nearby, was still in business with its gardens and orchard blooming, although the last vestiges of rural life west of the River Lea were soon to be built over in the next few years. The coming of the London and Blackwall Railway in 1840 supplied a great impetus to the industrial transformation of the area.[31]

The firm prospered and within a few years occupied three riverside sites covering an area of 5.67ha (14 acres) (Fig 19). The company began building small iron paddle steamers of 50–100 tons; so great was the reputation of Ditchburn and his revolutionary designs that orders were very soon coming in from all over the world.

The first iron ship produced by the new firm Ditchburn and Mare was the little fighting ship, *Inkerman*, built for the Russian navy to hunt out pirates operating in the Black Sea at the time (a forerunner of the international naval orders that would do so much to sustain the Thames Iron Works in its later years).[32]

Ditchburn persistently sought to persuade the Admiralty to introduce iron ships into the navy. In 1845 he was approached by the Admiralty 'as to the most proper size and form of vessel in which to convey her majesty from Whitehall to Woolwich'.[33] His proposal to use an Archimedean screw propeller (a still novel form of steam propulsion at the time, with most powered boats being paddle steamers), to 'screw her majesty from Whitehall to Woolwich, as one of their lordships remarked, was very like high treason'.[34] The result was Her Majesty's Yacht *Fairy* (Fig 20), which became a favourite of Queen Victoria and exceeded its original brief, serving as a coastal and cross-channel vessel in addition to a river yacht and tender to the royal yacht HMY *Victoria and Albert*. Charles Mare turned down a knighthood offered in recognition of the success of HMY *Fairy*; there may have been pressure on Mare due to his young age and relatively modest background to gracefully decline. It has been suggested that had Mare accepted the knighthood he might have found greater assistance when he ran into financial troubles with the yard in the mid 1850s.

Ditchburn's persistence regarding iron ships for the navy led to their requests for HMS *Trident*, an iron paddle sloop launched in December 1845, and HMS *Recruit*, a 12-gun iron-hulled sailing brig of the Royal Navy, launched in

1838

1855

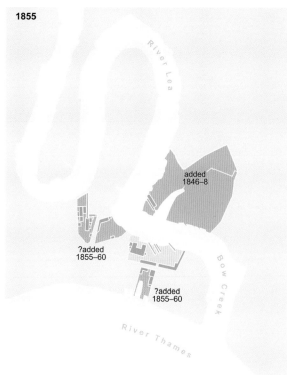

added
1846–8

?added
1855–60

?added
1855–60

slipway
new building
retained building
new area
retained area

1862

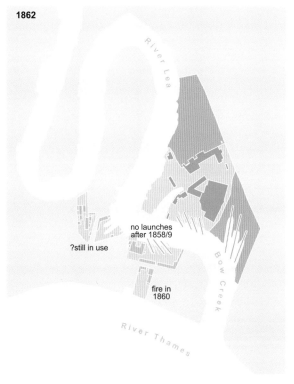

?still in use

no launches
after 1858/9

fire in
1860

1867

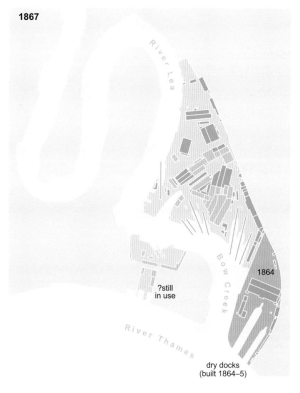

1864

?still
in use

dry docks
(built 1864–5)

THE THAMES IRON WORKS 1837–1912

N

travelling cranes
(built 1892–5)

1895

1895–1902

offices
(vacated 1903)

250m

1846. The two seem to have been the earliest iron-hulled vessels to be built for the Admiralty. HMS *Recruit* was the Royal Navy's only ever iron-hulled sailing ship, but there was still a great reluctance regarding iron ships at the Admiralty and she was sold back to her builders in 1849.[35]

Ditchburn and Mare became a leading name in the provision of steamers on the Thames, though at the time only a small yard. Some of their shipbuilding was still conducted using wood, although iron was increasingly used to create ship hulls or used in part to provide the structural elements of wooden-hulled vessels. These composite boats of part iron, part wood, were a solution to some of the structural issues raised by steam propulsion. The vessels produced by Ditchburn and Mare were becoming increasingly large and started to outstrip the capacity of the yard, both in terms of the size of the slips and number: '… at one period so great was the demand for space for which to lay down a keel, that a small up-river steamer was actually built inside a large sea-going one, the stern frames of the large one being left open that the small one might be launched through the opening'.[36]

With a lack of space on the Middlesex bank inhibiting further development, Mare resolved to expand on to the totally undeveloped Essex bank opposite the yard. He also determined that the new yard should possess the means of

Fig 19 (facing and above) The development of the Thames Iron Works and the preceding companies, 1838–1913 (based on the Charles Warner map (1913); LMA, ACC/2423/X/289 (1848–52); TNA, BT 356/11536 (1862), IR 30/12/154 (1852), IR 29/12/154 (1852); *Engineer* 1895, 567–77; OS 1867, 1894 and 1913–15; LCC 1994b, 674) (scale 1:10,000)

Fig 20 Painting of HMY
Fairy by George Mears
(Sworders Fine Art Auctioneers)

making its own iron, thereby negating the expense of buying and transporting prefabricated iron from elsewhere. Mare intended to capitalise on the relatively cheap and readily available waste iron being produced by London in large volumes. One spur for the expansion to the Essex bank was probably the coming into effect of the Metropolitan Buildings Act of 1844, the first of many measures to limit the effect of polluting and toxic industries within London. No such law existed just a few yards away on the Essex side of the Lea. Mare also probably wanted to capitalise on the impending coming of the railway to the Essex shore – a proposal of 1833 to extend the railway from Limehouse to 'a point in East Ham opposite Woolwich came to nothing but ten years later another scheme, promoted primarily to move seaborne coal from the riverside to places on the Eastern Counties Railway, was more successful'.[37] Seaborne coal was much cheaper than that transported by rail. The proximity to the new railway meant that Mare could be delivered scrap iron and coal – the raw ingredients of the new enterprise – almost directly into the yard. In 1844 an act of Parliament was passed and the line to Thames Wharf subsequently opened for freight in April 1846. 'Coke ovens were set up at Thames Wharf to convert sea coal into locomotive fuel for the Eastern Counties Railway and Northern & Eastern Railway'.[38] In that same year, 1846, C J Mare and Company began on the east bank also, with the laying down of eight small steamers for the Citizen Company, having evidently acquired land in anticipation of the coming railway.[39]

The year 1846 marks the beginning of the parting of ways for Ditchburn and Mare, at the height of their success. The reasons for the separation are not entirely clear, although Mackrow speculates that the rupture was caused by

THE THAMES IRON WORKS 1837–1912

Mare's proposal to expand the business into the marshes of the Essex bank.[40] Despite the imminent arrival of the railway, the land chosen by Mare did not seem ideally suited as the site for an industrial concern on the scale suggested. Almost the entire footprint of the planned yard was inundated by spring tides. The embankment which protected the land to the east curved away from the river at the northernmost point of the new yard before rejoining the bank to the south, encircling land hitherto considered too low lying and marshy to warrant protection. 'At the date of the first foundation of what is now the Thames Iron Works, one could look across them and see the traffic in the Mile End Road. At high spring tides, half the present shipyard premises were under water, and the land on first being taken up for shipbuilding purposes was covered with rushes as high as a man's waist'.[41] Mackrow, who was sent across the Lea to stake out two new slips, called the area 'Frog Island'.[42] While work was undertaken to prepare the new shipyard, in the distance the railway was being constructed on a dazzling bed of chalk to raise it above the marsh. Perhaps predictably, the opening of the railway was delayed by flooding during its construction.[43]

There are rumours of further strife in the relationship, with Mackrow stating that 'Mr Mare … spent his money as fast, or faster than he made it' and suggesting that as Mare 'was a gentleman who bred and ran horses for the turf, it may not be a very great stretch of the imagination to conceive money going out in that direction'.[44] The sheer cost of the new yard may have seemed to Ditchburn a reckless gamble. Arnold states that the usual capital outlay for iron shipbuilders was c £25,000.[45] In 1856, it was revealed that the 'Blackwall property, consisting of freehold and leasehold buildings, plant and machinery, had cost £225,000, although not all of this was spent at the outset'.[46] This is equivalent to approximately £13,169,250 in 2005.[47]

The degree to which the relationship soured is sadly demonstrated in court proceedings of 1848. The business had been formally dissolved on 1 May 1847 with a goodwill payment made to Ditchburn of £21,500,[48] though Ditchburn and Mare may have further cooperated for a time, with *The Times* commenting that the dissolution did not occur until September.[49] On dissolution, it was decided that an outstanding contract with Russia for a vessel of '1200 tons burden'[50] (possibly the wooden paddle steamer sloop *Vladimir*, 1680 displacement tons,[51] although *The Times* describes the ship as an 'iron steam vessel') would be finished by Mare. The Russian government was not happy with the stern of the ship and asked Ditchburn to observe Mare's work, which was being undertaken off site at Pilcher's (?Pitcher's) dock. On what was to be his final visit, on 9 April 1848, Ditchburn found his way barred by a certain Mr Gully who pushed over the ladder Ditchburn was on. The ladder fell 14ft (4.27m) and landed on Ditchburn.[52] It was stated by the prosecution that Mr Gully had been ordered not to allow Ditchburn access and was afterwards told by Mare that it would have been £50 for him had Ditchburn broken his neck; Mr Gully received a sovereign regardless.[53] In the end, Gully claimed that the sovereign was wages and it could not be proven that he had been given money by Mare for deliberately injuring Ditchburn. Gully was merely fined, Mare apologised and Ditchburn went away – a sorry end to such a fruitful relationship.

One outcome of these events was that Russia seems to have withdrawn its support of Mare's new yard – C J Mare and Company (below, 3.2). Ditchburn had a close relationship with the Russians, having built for them for 20 years and as clients they may have left with him.[54] No further Russian warships would be built on the Lea until the *Pervenetz* in 1863,[55] by which time Mare himself had long since departed (below, 3.3).

Ditchburn may have drifted away from shipbuilding after his retirement from the yard although he appears to have built at least one later vessel at a yard in Blackwall, the schooner yacht *Volna* in 1848 for the Grand Duke Constantine of Russia. For this he was presented with a 'splendid ring, bearing the Imperial Crown and the Grand Duke's initials, wrought in diamonds, on an enamelled shield of garter blue, surrounded with twelve large diamonds of the first water'.[56] Arnold states that Ditchburn continued with minor shipbuilding and some design, although by 1856 he was building houses locally.[57] As late as the 1861 census, his occupation was still given as 'Naval Architect'.[58] He died in 1870 but was survived by his wife, Helen, who was still residing at 153 East India Dock Road in 1871, a stone's throw from the yard that her husband had helped to make such a success.[59]

3.2 C J Mare and Company (1846/7–55)

Mare quickly established a yard that was capable of building ships weighing 2000–4000 tons. Four small steamers were built for the Citizen Company on each of the two new slips that Mackrow had staked out and all had been launched by the time the railway was completed in 1846.[60]

The task of reclaiming the marsh and building the new yard was immense. Mare dealt with the problem of the unstable ground by piling down 20ft (6.10m) to the underlying gravels. The timber piles were used across the whole of the new yard beneath walls and heavy structures. The task of creating the yard probably took around three years as the tonnage produced by the yard was lower in the years 1847–50 than it had been in the last full year of Ditchburn and Mare. However, business boomed from 1850 with output double that of even the peak years of Ditchburn and Mare.[61] Orders flooded into the new yard, with the majority being commercial steamers and foreign orders, while one fifth of the yard's output was for the Admiralty.[62] In 1853 alone, 43 vessels of various types and for various nations were on the stocks, ranging from little coal lighters to major ships.[63]

The yard was now an exemplar of a vertically integrated business – able to carry out almost all of the production sequence in-house with the newest tools and industrial machinery available,[64] including huge steam hammers, of the type designed by James Nasmyth[65] and capable of exerting a force of 90 tons (800.7kN) to shape iron (Chapter 2.2; Fig 14).

The yard also included puddling or ball furnaces for turning the scrap into useful iron, forges and rolling mills, along with all manner of steam-powered machinery for pressing, shaping, cutting and punching metal (Chapter 2.2).[66] The map of 1848–52 (Fig 21) shows the area Mare acquired on the Essex bank.[67] Although it does not show the internal arrangement of buildings within the new yard, it is likely that much of this area was occupied by industrial buildings by the early 1850s (Fig 19, 1855). While the OS map of 1867 shows the shipyard with its expansions in the 1860s, the footprint of Mare's original yard can be clearly seen as the densely packed industrial core, crowded with buildings right to the edge of the original space (Fig 19, 1862, 1867; cf Fig 27). A view of 1854 shows Bow Creek, looking south towards the Thames (Fig 22). The slips of C J Mare and Company can be seen fully occupied on both sides of the river, and on the left side, a large contained mass of industrial buildings can be seen to the east (left) of the occupied slips.

Fig 21 Detail from a map of 1848–52 'Navigation and river from the Thames (at Limehouse and Bow Creek) to Lea Bridge: part 2, Bow Creek to Four Mills (sheet 16)'; the Orchard Yard site and the expansion on to the Essex bank are outlined (scale 1:5000) (London Metropolitan Archives, City of London, ACC/2423/X/289)

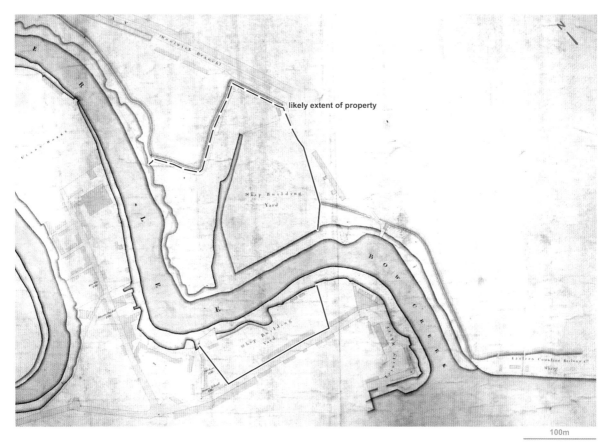

likely extent of property

100m

Fig 22 C J Mare and Company and Bow Creek, 1854, view looking (east) downriver from one of two inlets visible on the map in Fig 21 on the Middlesex bank opposite the spit of land known as 'Frog Island' (*ILN*, 28 October 1854, 409)

(Newham Heritage Service)

Another illustration from 1854 (Fig 23) shows the interior of a large working building. It is difficult to know how accurate the representation is, but it does illustrate a number of industrial processes taking place in the yard. In the background of the picture a large machine is silhouetted against an explosion of flames and sparks. This is possibly one of the steam hammers at the works. Mare had six of these by 1851, along with two rolling mills.[68] In the foreground of Fig 23, a large assortment of metal is heaped in front of a furnace (to the left), probably a puddling furnace, for turning it into iron blooms ready for rolling into plates. Barry writes that the work of gathering the bits of waste metal into piles, visible in the foreground of the illustration, was frequently undertaken by women.[69]

The yard did not limit itself to building ships but branched out into civil engineering. The step was an obvious one, as the iron created and the machinery employed by the yard could be applied just as well for land-based structures as it could for ship frames and plates. Sometimes the yard would work in conjunction with established specialist civil engineering firms. For the Britannia tubular bridge over the Menai Strait, between Anglesey and the mainland of Wales, C J Mare and Company provided the iron for Westwood and Baillie, 'experienced frame benders', to produce the tubular sections under subcontract.[70]

THE THAMES IRON WORKS 1837–1912

The difficulty of having the yard split across either side of the river (Fig 19, 1855) was solved by the creation of jetties and a chain ferry capable of carrying 200 people.[71] The old part of the yard on the Middlesex bank was used primarily for the building of smaller wooden ships. It was also the official address of the company and would continue to house the offices until the beginning of the 20th century (below, 3.3).

Given the seeming tremendous success of Mare's gamble in Essex, it is not clear why C J Mare and Company failed. The bankrupting of the yard in 1855 has been ascribed to a number of pressures and factors.[72] The Crimean War had a very great effect on Mare's business with production costs increasing dramatically, although the demand for vessels from the Admiralty brought huge amounts of work to many of the Thames private yards (Fig 24). Mare seems already to have been under some financial pressure in 1853. A measure to reduce costs by lowering wages from 6s 2d a day to 5s 8d a day resulted in strikes and the loss of 450 carpenters and joiners[73] out of a workforce totalling over 3000.[74] C J Mare and Company seem to have still been able to outdo some naval dockyards, however, as 22 shipwrights left Devonport (Devon) for Bow Creek on the offer of 6s a day and constant work for three years (an increase of 10s a week).[75] Wages shot up with production demands – shipwright wages on the Thames rising by 50% from June to October 1855 alone.[76] Materials also became more expensive. The winter of 1854/5 did not help as the

Fig 23 View showing the inside of one of the large buildings at C J Mare and Company at its height in 1854 (*ILN*, 28 October 1854, 409) (Newham Heritage Service)

Fig 24 British warships
in Cossack Bay,
Balaklava (Crimean
Peninsula), in the mid
1850s
(photograph by Roger Fenton;
Royal Photographic Society/
National Media Museum/
Science & Society Picture
Library)

Thames froze over, impeding both coal supply and also making the launching of any ships impossible.

Part of the problem faced by Mare was that much of the work they undertook was at fixed price contract. With fairly tight margins, the possibility of a profit being transformed by changing conditions into a significant loss was high. The company was experiencing huge losses on some of its civil work, in particular, the Royal Albert Bridge, being built over the Tamar between Plymouth and Saltash (Cornwall), and Westminster Bridge, in the City of London; the latter had been won for the yard on an exceedingly low agreed cost.[77] The tipping point appears to have been the production of six wooden gunboats for the Admiralty.[78] These boats – originally ordered as despatch boats before being redesignated gunboats – were supposed to have brought the company £10,000 but instead were costing the yard 'much more'.[79] Banbury, however, stresses that the oversight on the gunboats alone cannot have sunk the yard.[80]

Mare placed at least a portion of the blame with some of his customers, stating that the difficulties 'arose from the delay in payment of debts due to him for work performed'.[81] Theft in the yard was highlighted by the *ILN* as a particular problem and suggested that several marine store dealers, who also closed in the aftermath of C J Mare and Company passing, may have been fences for materials taken from the yard, stating that 'the property stolen from the works was estimated at some thousands of pounds per annum'.[82]

After losing control of his yard on the Lea (below, 3.3), Charles Mare went to manage W and H Pitcher at Northfleet when it failed in 1857, possibly to help the company wind down its production, with the yard finally closing in 1861. That year, Mare, took control of Scott Russell's former yard that had launched the *Great Eastern* and renamed it the Millwall Iron Works. As with the Thames Iron Works (below, 3.3), the yard produced its own iron and ran successfully in competition with it for several years. Business was steady, but the enterprise came to a catastrophic end with the failure to launch HMS *Northumberland*. The ship had spent five years on the stocks due to constant revisions to the design and when finally launched she stuck on the lower portion of the slipway, remaining there for four weeks until four 'wooden *camels* or immense tanks … made at Woolwich Dockyard' finally lifted the vessel free.[83] The failed launch cost at least £12,000, effectively sinking the yard and in part helping to foment the collapse of one of the greatest financial institutions in the history of the City, Overend, Gurney and Company, in 1866. The breaking of Overend, Gurney and Company precipitated a national financial depression and the further closure of several yards on the Thames.[84] Shipbuilding on the Thames never recovered.[85]

Charles Mare epitomises the era in which he lived, coming to prominence during a time of great industrial speculation and growth. His financial overreaching and eventual demise in many ways mirrors that of Thames shipbuilding in the 1850s and 1860s, and his withdrawal from public life echoes the disappearance of many of the previously successful Thames shipbuilders and the moribund state of shipbuilding in the decades following the crash of 1866. His successes and failures were of truly epic proportions. Mackrow writes of Mare with 'the fondest regard, as being … in his youthful days the very ideal of a gentleman and for whose sad, sad evening of life he feels the deepest sorrow'.[86] Charles Mare died, his vast wealth gone, in Stepney, in 1898. The obituary in the *TIWG* describes how Mare's wife, the elderly and ailing Mary, placed with her departed husband a small bunch of barley, which he had presented to her half a century before and which she had treasured all the long years of their marriage.[87] This tender act seems a fitting tribute to the rural background of a figure who played such a great part in the transformation of east London from rustic marshland to industrial leviathan.

3.3 Thames Iron Works and Shipbuilding Company Limited (1856–1912)

In 1856, control of the shipyard, which creditors were keen to see maintained as it was still a viable business, passed to Mare's father-in-law, Peter Rolt (Fig 25). Mackrow suggests that Mare was already heavily mortgaged to Rolt and it seems probable that the business had been propped up for some time.[88] Rolt stepped down from Parliament to take over the directorship of the reformed

Fig 25 Portrait of Peter Rolt (*TIWG*, no. 14, 1898, 55)

(National Maritime Museum, Greenwich, London, 629.12)

Fig 26 A page from the inside cover of the 1863 prospectus showing the original shareholders at the inception of the Thames Iron Works as a limited company

(National Maritime Museum, Greenwich, London, 629.12)

shipyard, incorporated in 1857 as the Thames Iron Works and Shipbuilding Company Limited.[89] The objective of the company was 'the building of ships, forging, casting and rolling of iron, the construction of wrought and cast ironwork generally, and all such works and business as may be incident thereto'.[90] The new company was formed with the advantage of personal financial protections afforded by the new Limited Liability Act of 1855 (18 and 19 Vict, c 133) and the Joint Stock Companies Act of 1856 (19 and 20 Vict, c 47), personal liability being limited only to the amount represented by the shares held. Mare had been liable to the whole extent of his private property. The passing of these acts 'gave an enormous impulse to the promotion of public companies'.[91] There were 20 shares of £5000 each. While Rolt had five shares, it is interesting to note the name of the Deptford chemical industrialist, Frank Hills (Fig 26), who would later come to be a major shareholder in the yard.

NAMES AND ADDRESSES OF SUBSCRIBERS.		Number of Shares taken by each Subscriber.
George Frederick Blumberg	17, Norfolk Villas, Westbourne Grove, in the County of Middlesex	One.
John Bonus	18, Cannon Street, in the City of London	One.
D. Stewart Dykes	Grove Hill, Camberwell, in the County of Surrey	One.
Henry Edwards	Denmark Hill, in the County of Surrey	One.
Joshua Field	Lambeth, in the County of Surrey	One.
John Ford	4, Oakley Villas, Adelaide Road, Hampstead, in the County of Middlesex	One.
Edward Godson	72, Aldersgate Street, in the City of London	One.
F. C. Hills	Chemical Works, Deptford, in the County of Kent	Two.
John Kelk	South Street, Grosvenor Square, in the County of Middlesex	Two.
Thomas Henry Maudslay	Lambeth, in the County of Surrey	One.
Henry Maudslay	Lambeth, in the County of Surrey	One.
Thos. Henry Maudslay, Jun.	Clapham Road, in the County of Surrey	One.
Peter Rolt	4, Clement's Lane, in the City of London	Five.
Edward Vigers	23, Upper Lisson Street, in the County of Middlesex	One.
	Total Shares taken	Twenty.

Dated the Twenty-second day of December, 1856.

Witness to the above Signatures,
JAMES HOLAH,
Clerk to Messrs. Newbon, Evans, & Newbon, Solicitors,
1, Wardrobe Place, Doctor's Commons, In the City of London.

The Thames Iron Works and Shipbuilding Company became the largest and most important shipbuilding company on the River Thames. The majority of the work was undertaken on the site on the east bank of the River Lea, which expanded from roughly 4.25ha (10½ acres) in the early 1850s to occupy just under 11ha (27 acres) by 1912. Much of this expansion took place in the first years of the new company with 9.7ha (24 acres) already occupied by 1863 (cf Fig 19; Fig 27).[92]

One of the new yard's early contracts was for HMS *Warrior* (1860), which, when commissioned on 1 August 1861, was the largest ironclad warship in the world.[93] HMS *Warrior* was also the first capital ship built for the Royal Navy by a private firm (Fig 28).

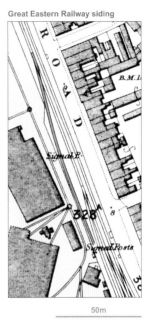

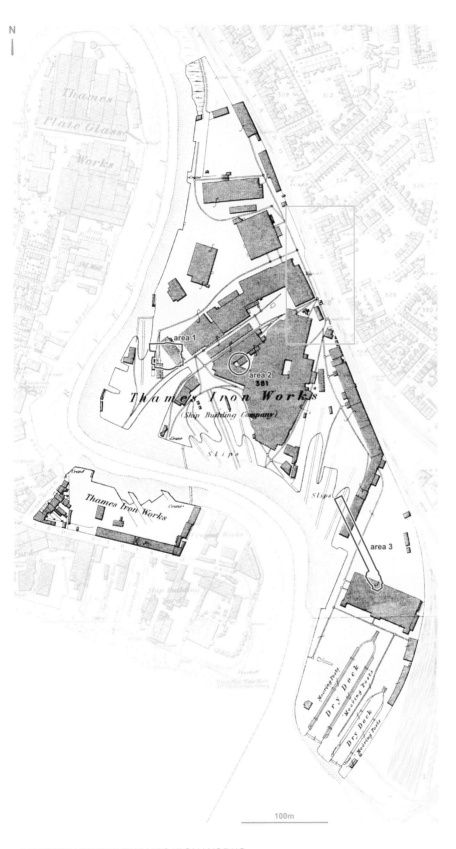

50m

Fig 27 Extract from the 1867 OS map showing the Thames Iron Works at its greatest extent on the Essex side of the River Lea with the areas of investigation superimposed; (inset) detail showing the Great Eastern Railway siding (in red) from which materials were transferred to the internal tramway in the yard (scale 1:4250; inset, 1:2125)

100m

The building of this ship was the first time that many separate, previously tested elements had come together in a warship of such size. HMS *Warrior* possessed an iron hull, was steam-powered and screw-propelled, although she also retained masts and a ship rig sail arrangement. One innovation, though never again employed, was the tongue and groove arrangement of her wrought iron armour plate, produced in the steam hammers (which by this time numbered seven)[94] at the yard from scrap. The *Warrior* was conceived in response to the French warship *Gloire*, launched in 1859.[95] The *Gloire* was the first ocean-going ironclad in the world, although she still possessed a wooden hull. The Thames Iron Works lost around £61,400 on the *Warrior* due to the problems of executing such an innovative vessel.[96] While the yard made a literal loss on the ship, the value to the increased reputation of the yard cannot be measured. Further Admiralty orders would follow as Thames Iron Works became increasingly known as a builder of warships, and foreign powers came to the yard to have ships built as close to Admiralty specifications as possible (Table 1).

The year 1860 was also the beginning of a new phase of expansion for the yard. In early September the yard on the Middlesex bank suffered a terrible fire, which destroyed large parts of their premises there, including 'sawing, moulding and planning mills, smithies and the like, replete with a system of elaborate and costly machinery, all of which was driven by a steam engine of some 60-horse power'.[97] The fire caused damage upwards of £10,000, with

Fig 28 HMS *Warrior* being built on the main slip at the Thames Iron Works; the slipway was the central of the upper slips, with the lower slips being added later in the life of the yard (*ILN*, 29 December 1860, 634)

(Look and Learn, U321803)

THE THAMES IRON WORKS 1837–1912

the loss also of large quantities of the finest timber. All work on timbers for the *Warrior* was being undertaken on the Middlesex bank, with the components being taken across to the *Warrior*'s slip. Land was acquired to extend operations on the Essex bank and those on the Middlesex bank wound down over the next few years (Fig 19). Some activities continued on the Middlesex bank, with Barry reporting in 1863 that there were still plumbers' shops and timber yards there,[98] although no ships appear to have been launched from the Middlesex bank after the Royal Mail Steam Packet Company ship *Paramatta* in 1858 or 1859.[99] The leases on much of the property on the Middlesex side were not renewed on their expiry in 1867, with that retained only being renewed annually,[100] although a small area was retained under lease until 1903 as the site of the company's registered offices.[101]

The scale of expansion can be seen in a plan of 1862 (Fig 19, 1862),[102] drawn to illustrate the rebuilding of an embankment to the north of Mare's old yard. The embankment was constructed to raise the riverbank and build a protective wall to shield the newly acquired area to the east. The land was probably acquired in 1861, as the large new foundry building was built then with the old foundry becoming a smiths' shop. Also built were a new sawmill and a range of buildings purely for the civil engineering department in the north of the yard on the site of houses previously occupied by the coke burners' working ovens south of the yard.[103] In 1861 the *Mechanics' Magazine* chose the Thames Iron Works to open a serial on the 'Leviathan workshops' of the capital,[104] the others being Rennies, Lambeth Distillery, Enfield Small Arms Factory and De La Rue (who still make banknotes for the Bank of England today).[105] The magazine described the Thames Iron Works as being, 'of the true cyclopean type … a constant rumbling and reverberation … with foundry and furnace flames … the black breathings of Vulcan's nostrils'.[106]

South of Mare's old yard, three new slipways were built on land acquired around the same time (Fig 19, 1862). The 1862 map still shows it occupied by the Northumberland and Durham Coal Company;[107] however, the map may not have been updated to show the new southern area and may have been drawn from older information. The Marsh Authorities compelled the Thames Iron Works to rebuild the river defences to pass around the north end of the new slips,[108] as they were concerned about the risk to flooding of Canning Town, Newham (formerly Essex), which was in parts 14ft (4.27m) below high water. At the south-east limit of the early 1860s expansion, a new mast house and mould loft was built in 1862, as the previous one had been destroyed by fire in December 1861. Due to the worries of the Marsh Authorities regarding flooding, a veto was placed on any works that might interfere with the newly constructed river wall just to the east of the southernmost slipway and Mackrow explains that this resulted in the overhang of the mould loft on the west side of the new building. The building was erected with the piles along that edge driven free of the river wall.[109] (For archaeological evidence: Chapter 4.3.)

Nationally, shipbuilding experienced a boom in the years leading up to the financial crash and fall of the bankers Overend and Gurney, in 1866.[110] During this period, Thames Iron Works sought to capitalise by extending its premises again *c* 1864. On this extension, to the south of the yard, a major building devoted to marine engineering was built and equipped with the newest machinery. The building was afterwards referred to as the 'engineering building' and was a showcase for the company, with a frontage visible to all who used the Thames (Fig 29). A huge amount was also invested in two dry docks 'built of solid masonry at great cost', one 460ft (140.20m) long and capable of taking in the largest ships of the day.[111] The company was reformed as Thames Iron Works Shipbuilding Engineering and Dry Dock Company Limited in 1864 (Fig 27).[112] The reorganisation was needed in part to fund the new ship repair enterprise, finished at a cost of £85,000 in 1865,[113] but also to address financial difficulties that the yard found itself in, with liabilities greater than its share capital.

There was a great drop-off in commercial shipbuilding on the Thames around this time, with much of the available work going to the northern shipbuilders. The production of ocean mail steamers and passenger liners on the Thames all but ceased in 1865.[114] Peninsula and Oriental Steam Navigation Company, who had previously placed several of its orders with Thames Iron Works, saw their last launch from Blackwall, the *Tanjour*, that year.[115] The Thames as a whole had suffered increasingly in competition from the northern firms, who were unburdened by a number of financial concerns faced by shipbuilders on the Thames. These included higher rates in London, higher

Fig 29 The engineering building as seen from the contemporary dry docks fronting the River Thames, view looking north-east (photograph published in *Engineer* 1895, 567 fig 1)
(Graces Guides)

THE THAMES IRON WORKS 1837–1912

wages and a degree of organisation of workers' interests (Chapter 5) which did not exist in the North, particularly in Scotland, where the workforce was seen as much more malleable to business concerns. The northern yards were also closer to the raw materials.[116]

Following the 1866 financial crash, the Thames Iron Works experienced years of downturn and hardship. Charles Mare's new enterprise, the Millwall Iron Works, with whom the Thames Iron Works competed in the recovery years after the post-Crimean War slump, had gone bankrupt that year. Without commercial trade and as increasingly specialised builders, the Thames Iron Works spent several years scraping by; it launched only three commercial vessels larger than 1000 displacement tons over the last 46 years of its life, compared to 15 alone in the previous decade with all but four of these being over 2500 displacement tons.[117] Of these, one was an experimental twin-hulled steamer, the *Castalia*, laid down in 1873, and the second, the *Invicta*, a channel steamer, in 1882. The third was a prototype 1000 ton coaling lighter designed by Mackrow and built by the yard in 1904, but never put into production. Oil was increasingly being considered as a power source for seagoing vessels. By 1900 it had become accepted practice to spray oil on to coal to increase combustion. In Britain 'the development of (solely) oil-fired ships was promoted by Admiral John Fisher, First Sea Lord from 1904 to 1910'.[118]

With difficulties extending into the 1870s, further reorganisations of the company were required, with the company being reincorporated as the short-lived Thames Ship Building Graving Docks and Iron Works Company Limited in 1871.[119] Work was inconsistent and the workforce dramatically reduced in number to 1100,[120] compared with a peak of 5000–6000 in the years leading up to 1866,[121] although the yard was still producing ships of over 2500 tons, mostly warships for the Turkish and British governments.[122] The yard was reincorporated yet again as the Thames Iron Works and Ship Building Company Limited in 1872.[123] That year the ironworks acquired the powerful rolling mill from Mare's defunct Millwall Iron Works at scrap price and the engines converted from 'common to compound'.[124] The year 1872 also marked the transfer of the business to Frank Hills who had become the majority shareholder (Fig 30). The business was returning to being a more family-run enterprise. There were only eight shareholders in 1873, 'Lord Churchill, John Bulmer and six members of the Hills family'.[125] Arnold Hills, Frank's son, would join the board in 1880,[126] taking over effective running of the yard in the mid 1880s and heading it to the end. Frank Hills may have remained chairman until his death[127] in May 1892.[128]

Fig 30 Portrait of Frank Clark Hills who had made his fortune in Deptford as an industrial chemicals producer
(Newham Heritage Service)

The years following a brief upturn in the middle part of the 1870s were very hard for Thames Iron Works. The shipbuilding department subsisted on a series of smaller vessels, mostly under 1000 displacement tons, although with the occasional larger vessels, such as the cruisers *Gravina* and *Velasco* (both 1139 displacement tons), laid down in 1881 for the Spanish government, and HMS *Benbow* (10,011 displacement tons) in 1882 and HMS *Sans Pareil* (10,538 displacement tons) (Fig 70) in 1885 for the British.[129] The commercial trade was limited almost entirely to very minor vessels, many of which were under 100 displacement tons.[130] The Thames Iron Works was of a size far more suited to the steady production of a large number of medium to large vessels and the yard suffered terribly, with parts of the yard almost idle and widespread unemployment in the area.[131]

Thames Iron Works was still sought out by those requiring unusual or specialist vessels, as the yard maintained its status as innovators. One very unusual request of 1877 was for a vessel to transport Cleopatra's Needle from Egypt to London. The vessel was designed by John Dixon, a civil engineer in London (Fig 31). The ironworks created several iron rings within which the obelisk was encased on site in Alexandria and packed in wood (Fig 32). Once secure, it was rolled down the beach and packed inside the cylinder-shaped vessel, the *Cleopatra*, to be towed back to London by the steamer *Olga*. The operation worked well and the vessels made good progress, passing through the Strait of Gibraltar, before coming into serious trouble in a terrible storm in the Bay of Biscay in mid October 1877. The tow line snapped and following attempts to reconnect it, which cost six lives, the *Cleopatra* was abandoned (Fig 33). It floated around the Atlantic for a time until it was eventually rediscovered by Spanish trawlers and towed by the Glasgow steamer *Fitzmaurice* into Ferrol, on Spain's north coast, for repairs.[132] Following the negotiation of a hefty £2000 salvage fee with the master of the *Fitzmaurice*, *Cleopatra* left, being towed by the tug *Anglia* up the Thames to arrive in London in January 1878 where, following much debate, it was placed on the Victoria Embankment where it stands today. The durability of the vessel that carried the obelisk is testament to the quality of workmanship in the yard, and perhaps spared the

Fig 31 Cylinder ship *Cleopatra*, 1877 (Mackrow 1900, 112)
(by permission of Durham University Library)

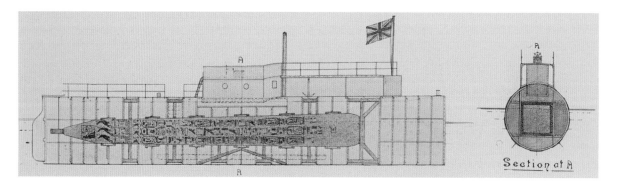

Section at A

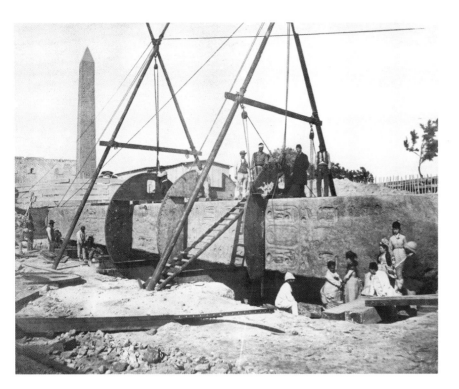

Fig 32 Erecting the rings and digging out below the obelisk on the shore at Alexandria (Egypt) (National Maritime Museum, Greenwich, London, L5584)

bafflement of future generations of marine archaeologists had the vessel foundered. The enterprise did not, however, make much money for the yard – 'for such a laudable object, the Directors did not look to make a large profit out of the transaction'.[133]

Thames Iron Works was given a great reprieve by the Naval Defence Act of 1889, which formalised the country's 'two power standard'. The standard implied that Britain should maintain a naval strength equal to the two next largest naval powers; it had been Britain's policy 'to keep up a navy equal to the navies of any two powers that can be brought against us' since at least 1817.[134] Of the orders for eight first-class battleships, two second-class battleships, 42 cruisers of various classes and 18 torpedo boats, several came to the yard.[135]

In 1899 the Thames Iron Works was reformed again as Thames Iron Works Shipbuilding and Engineering Company Limited[136] and acquired John Penn and Sons, the famous, though by contemporary standards, fairly small engineers and engine builders (Chapter 2.1). The company took on further debts to

Fig 33 The *Cleopatra* adrift (Mackrow 1900, 113) (by permission of Durham University Library)

Fig 34 Men and machinery in 1901; the triangular frame in the background (top right) suggests the picture is taken at John Penn and Sons

(Newham Heritage Service)

secure the reformed company, update the facilities, particularly at Penn and Sons, and create working capital (Fig 34).[137]

The previous years had seen a number of large warships built both for Britain and Japan, and it was assumed that further orders would come to Thames Iron Works. In 1899, the dry docks were very busy, as was the civil engineering department, and there was engagement of other work across much of the yard. Two battleships, HMS *Duncan* and HMS *Cornwallis*, were on the company's slipways.[138] The effort towards increasing the level of the company's vertical integration to make it more competitive with the northern firms, however, was probably a case of too little too late. With the boom of shipbuilding instigated by the Naval Defence Act of 1889 passing, orders dropped off.

The 1899 restructuring of the company did not provide enough working capital and in 1901 the company took on further debts. There was still an air of optimism, with it stated in the annual report in April 1900 'that in view of the magnitude of the company's existing contracts and their constantly increasing business, the recommendation of the Directors (to take on further debt for investment) … is hereby approved and referred … to a special meeting of the shareholders'.[139] The reinvestment in Thames Iron Works did not lead to the work that was hoped for, with the yard still seriously undercut by their northern competitors at tender.

THE THAMES IRON WORKS 1837–1912

The mergers occurring in the North were on a far grander scale, notably 'Vickers Barrow and Maxim, and Armstrong Mitchell with Whitworth'.[140] The northern mergers meant that the vast enterprises could easily acquire raw materials, being near to the coal fields and iron deposits, and in some cases having a financial interest in mining. They could produce the steel, build the ships and also arm them. Hills complained bitterly that the 'armaments ring', as the virtual monopolies became known, could unfairly undercut tenders from elsewhere, supplementing loss leaders on building ships with revenue from their armaments.[141] The government encouraged the formation of a third major arms consortium to compete with the northern firms and drive down prices, and the Coventry Ordnance Works Limited was established in 1905. However, this did little to aid the Thames shipbuilders, whose costs were still higher than those in the North, and they received very few orders from the Admiralty from 1900 onwards. Thames Iron Works itself received only four further orders for British warships from 1900 till their close in 1912, with only two of those significant ships – the armoured cruiser HMS *Black Prince* and battleship HMS *Thunderer*.[142]

A further setback to the competitiveness of Thames Iron Works had been caused (at least in Arnold Hills's opinion, writing in 1911) by the passing in 1891 of a House of Commons Fair Wages Resolution. The resolution was admirably conceived to 'prevent the evils of sweating' of the workforce and compelled the government contractor producing the ships under tender to pay 'the rate of wages current in his district'.[143] Unfortunately, this tied the Thames Iron Works to a 'handicap of some 5% (extra) upon the cost of all government contracts' in competition with the lower rates of the 'Provincial Outports'.[144] Hills argued that the higher wages should be accommodated by the Admiralty and work still be given to London despite the resulting higher tender, as the execution was of a higher quality. He also justified the right of London to be allowed to continue as a shipbuilder by the fact that the City generated tax revenue 'more than one fifth of the imperial revenue' and that the higher wages and costs of Thames Iron Works operating in the metropolis should be more than recompensed by this.[145] Hills did not go as far as directly appealing for a London-weighting subsidy, but only in name.

Totalling all the vessels made by Ditchburn and Mare, C J Mare and Company and the Thames Iron Works, the shipyard was responsible for producing at least 899 vessels including over 140 warships alone over the course of its life.[146] The yard was not confined to shipbuilding and, to make the most of transferable skills and facilities, added several related disciplines towards the end, in addition to the civil engineering, which had been a part of the yard's output since the days of C J Mare and Company. Shipbuilding and civil engineering were organised as departments, with other departments eventually being added, including electrical engineering, cranes and boatbuilding. The company also added a marine engines and motor car department, although it should be noted that this last department constituted the works of John Penn and Sons at Greenwich with marine engineering transferring to John Penn and Sons *c* 1900.[147]

Over the course of its life the civil engineering side of the business produced ironwork for several large projects and a wealth of smaller ones (Fig 35). Projects included the ribs for the domes of the International Exhibition Building in London (1862), the roof for the Royal Aquarium in the City of Westminster (opened 1876), Blackfriars railway bridge, City of London (opened 1886), and Hammersmith suspension bridge, in Hammersmith and Fulham (1883–7), ironwork for the Rotherhithe road tunnel (1904–8; Fig 36) and the gates for HM Dockyard at Devonport (1911) as well as numerous projects abroad such as the Kotri Bridge (1900) which still spans the Indus to Hyderabad in Pakistan.[148]

The ironworks redeveloped one of its slips, erecting three (wooden) boatbuilding facilities in its place (Fig 37). The largest of these buildings,

Fig 35 A selection of civil engineering projects undertaken at the Thames Iron Works (*TIWG*, no. 13, 1897, facing p 3)
(National Maritime Museum, Greenwich, London)

THE THAMES IRON WORKS 1837–1912

marked on the Charles Warner map as 'No.1 Boat Building Shed' (Fig 39), was equipped with four 'launching ways'. (These were among the last traces of shipbuilding to survive, and are visible at the very top of the aerial photograph of 1933 (Fig 101). The yard began building boats at the time of the *Fuji* being on its slips in 1895 'in consequence of being unable to find satisfactory wooden boats from outside'.[149] This would evolve into a significant part of its business, with the Thames Iron Works becoming sole supplier of lifeboats to the RNLI (Fig 38); 206 lifeboats were built for the

Fig 36 Caisson for the Rotherhithe Tunnel at the Thames Iron Works (Tower Hamlets Local History Library and Archives)

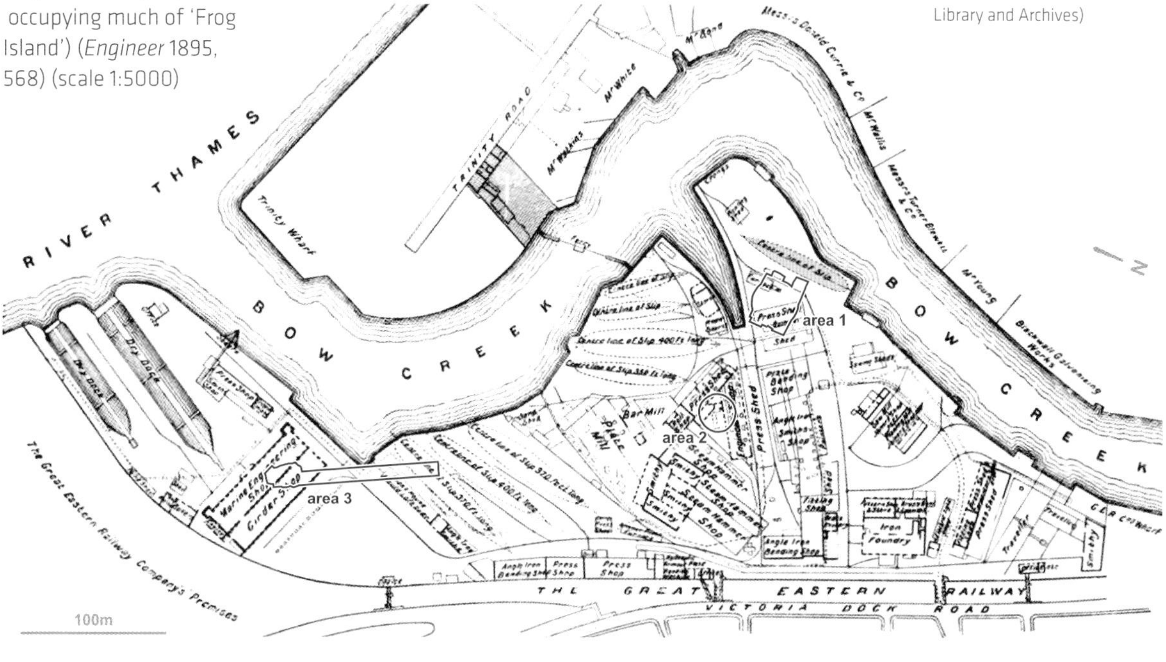

Fig 37 The map published in the *Engineer* which ran a long piece on the Thames Iron Works, describing its various areas via a walk-through (the slipway (highlighted) redeveloped for the new boatbuilding shed is the single northerly slip occupying much of 'Frog Island') (*Engineer* 1895, 568) (scale 1:5000)

Fig 38 The *Nancy Lucy*, a lifeboat built for the RNLI in 1903
(National Maritime Museum, Greenwich, London, N16992)

RNLI at the yard from 1896 until closure in 1912, with around 50 more internationally.

While the civil engineering department and some other areas maintained a relatively healthy amount of work, the shipbuilding and ship repairing sides of the business had very little. An almost indefatigable optimism still persisted. On the launch of HMS *Nautilus*, a torpedo boat destroyer of 1060 displacement tons, Hills hoped it would 'prove the precursor of a considerable revival in Shipbuilding on the Thames'.[150]

The extent to which the Thames Iron Works was forced to diversify is evident in the structure of the historical catalogue, which was prepared for the Festival of Empire, Crystal Palace, in 1911, and is not just a souvenir but very much a promotional catalogue.[151] Each of the departments is discussed and, while shipbuilding and marine engineering do occupy greater portions of the content, much weight is given to the other departments. The motor car section at the back resembles more an advertising brochure, with testimonials for each of the vehicles included (mostly written by owners with a vested interest).

Thames Iron Works had invested huge amounts of money to accommodate HMS *Thunderer* and gambled on further government orders, spending over £75,000 (approximately £4,279,500 in 2005, converted for the years 1900–10)[152] on a new crane and a fitting-out dock at Dagenham, Barking and Dagenham (formerly Essex). In the end perhaps Hills had isolated or upset too many people personally (Chapter 5) or the Thames Iron Works was seen as too problematic, as a tender in 1910 for one of two battleships to follow HMS *Thunderer* was overlooked, despite, according to Hills at least, being the cheapest by £5000 pounds and in apparent violation of the tendering policy.[153] The battleship contracts went to Messrs Scott of Greenock (Renfrewshire) on the Clyde (HMS *Ajax*) and Messrs Cammell and Laird on the Mersey (HMS *Audacious*).[154] HMS *Thunderer* had created a brief resurgence for the yard but after the launch in 1911 the banks refused to honour the company's cheques, and in November a receiver-manager was appointed on behalf of the debenture holders.[155]

The Admiralty had promised more work for Thames Iron Works, so long as the workers there abandon the eight-hour day, a concession which had been hard fought for and which had become a cornerstone of the yard's employment values. It is perhaps unsurprising that this was voted against and a potential management takeover by Vickers evaporated. Every effort was made by Hills to secure a future for the yard, but the First Debenture holders could not be persuaded to accept the proposed financial restructuring. The resolution was 'lost by a single vote' and the site closed in December of 1912.[156] Many have remarked that it seems strange that at the height of a naval shipbuilding boom, the Thames should be deprived of its last major shipbuilding concern and the nation of an industrial resource built on over 70 years of expertise.

Notes to Chapter 3

1 GRO, Christening Records, 1799; Births and Christenings, 1813, p 75 no. 599

2 *TIWG*, no. 15, 1898, 116

3 *Engineer* 1870, 265; Arnold 2000, 27

4 *TIWG*, no. 2, 1895, 40

5 Arnold 2000, 14

6 *TIWG*, no. 2, 1895, 40

7 Ibid

8 Dodd 1867, 174–5

9 Russell 1845, 13

10 Dodd 1858c, 16

11 *TIWG*, no. 2, 1895, 40

12 LMA, P93/DUN/73, 14 January 1837, 242

13 TNA, 1841 England Census

14 Banbury 1971, 164

15 GRO, Christening Records, 1814

16 *TIWG*, no. 15, 1898, 117

17 *Charles John Mare*

18 Ibid

19 *TIWG*, no. 1, 1895, 3

20 LMA, P87/JNE1, item 8

21 *TIWG*, no. 15, 1898, 118

22 Banbury 1971, 268

23 *General steam*; *P&O heritage*

24 SM, MS 616/1, 39–42; Banbury 1971, 194

25 *ILN*, 28 October 1854, 410

26 *TIWG*, no. 5, 1896, 15

27 Arnold 2000, 61

28 *TIWG*, no. 15, 1898, 118

29 Marshall 2013, 137

30 LCC 1994a

31 Timbs 1840, 225; Arnold 2000, 22

32 *TIWG*, no. 2, 1895, 40

33 Ibid, 42

34 Ibid

35 Colledge and Warlow 2010, 333

36 G Mackrow in *TIWG*, no. 2, 1895, 40

37 Jackson 1978, 175

38 Ibid

39 *TIWG*, no. 1, 1895, 3; SM, MS 616/1, 37

40 *TIWG*, no. 1, 1895, 3

41 *Engineer* 1894, 567

42 *TIWG*, no. 1, 1895, 3

43 Jackson 1978, 175

44 *TIWG*, no. 5, 1896, 2

45 Arnold 2000, 40

46 *Banking almanac* 1856, 52, quoted in Arnold 2000, 41

47 *Currency converter*

48 *The Times*, 7 June 1856, 11

49 *The Times*, 8 May 1848, 7

50 *The Times*, 21 July 1848, 7

51 SM, MS 616/1, 19

52 *The Times*, 21 July 1848, 7

53 Ibid

54 Ibid

55 SM, MS 616/1, 11 and 21

56 *ILN*, 18 November 1848, 311

57 Arnold 2000, 39

58 TNA, 1861 England Census

59 TNA, 1871 England Census; *Engineer* 1870, 265

60 *TIWG*, no. 1, 1895, 3

61 Arnold 2000, 42

62 Ibid

63 *TIWG*, no. 5, 1896, 2

64 Arnold 2000, 38

65 Ibid, 42

66 Ibid, 40

67 LMA, ACC/2423/X/289

68 *The Times*, 27 August 1851, 5

69 Barry 1863b, 65

70 Arnold 2000, 41

71 *TIWG*, no. 24, 1900, 164

72 Arnold 2000, 59–61

73 *Builder*, 17 December 1853

74 *The Times*, 4 April 1854, 9

75 *ILN*, 28 January 1854, 75

76 Arnold 2000, 52

77 *TIWG*, no. 15, 1898, 118

78 *TIWG*, no. 5, 1896, 3

79 Arnold 2000, 60

80 Banbury 1971, 196

81 *The Times*, 27 September 1855, 10

82 *ILN*, 19 September 1857, 287

83 *TIWG*, no. 6, 1896, 50

84 Arnold 2000, 67–8

85 Buxton 2012, 134

86 *TIWG*, no. 15, 1898, 118

87 Ibid

88 *TIWG*, no. 5, 1896, 2

89 TNA, BT 31/219/686

90 Ibid

91 G Mackrow in *TIWG*, no. 15, 1898, 116–17

92 Barry 1863b, 66

93 *Thames Iron Works*

94 Wells 1987, 35

95 Ibid, 15

96 *TIWG*, no. 2, 1895, 45

97 *The Times*, 3 September 1860, 10

98 Barry 1863a, 219

99 Arnold 2000, 62; *Ships list* b

100 Arnold 2000, 96

101 LMA, O/045, annual rep 1902

102 TNA, BT 356/11536

103 *TIWG*, no. 3, 1895, 45

104 *Mechanics' Mag* 1861

105 Rankin 2014

106 *Mechanics' Mag* 1861, 94

107 TNA, BT 356/11536

108 *TIWG*, no. 7, 1896, 93

109 Ibid

110 Arnold 2000, 66

111 *ILN*, 6 October 1866, 348

112 TNA, BT 31/913/1080C

113 Buxton 2004, 158

114 Banbury 1971, 69

115 Arnold 2000, 73

116 Ibid, 37

117 SM, MS 616/1, 41–5

118 Weissenbacher 2009, i, 373

119 TNA, BT 31/1597/5338

120 Arnold 2000, 109

121 Ibid, 95

122 SM, MS 616/1, 23

123 TNA, BT 31/1722/6293

124 *TIWG*, no. 15, 1898, 117

125 Arnold 2000, 112

126 Powles 2005, 5

127 Belton 2010, p 106

128 *The Times*, 5 May 1892, 1

129 SM, MS 616/1, 23–5

130 Ibid, 43–5

131 *TIWG*, no. 9, 1896, 2

132 Mackrow 1900, 114

133 Ibid, 115

134 Lord Castlereagh in *Hansard* 1848, 3 ser, xcvii, 779–80, quoted in Wells 1987, 12

135 SM, MS 616/1, passim; Arnold 2000, 124

136 LMA, ACC/1712/108; Arnold 2000, 140

137 Ibid

138 SM, MS 616/1, 7 and 25

139 LMA, O/045, 12

140 Rutterford 2007, 73

141 Arnold 2000, 147

142 SM, MS 616/1, 25

143 Hills 1911, 1

144 Ibid

145 Ibid

146 SM, MS 616/1, 5

147 Ibid

148 Ibid, 95–111

149 Ibid, 47

150 LMA, O/045, annual rep 1908

151 SM, MS 616/1

152 *Currency converter*

153 Hills 1911, 3

154 Ibid

155 Rutterford 2007, 81

156 Ibid, 82

CHAPTER 4

THE ARCHAEOLOGY OF THE THAMES IRON WORKS

The following discussion of the archaeological investigation of the site has been organised according to the areas of intervention (Fig 2). The three areas investigated included the evaluation trenches and main shaft (area 1), auxiliary shaft (area 2) and two trenches at Instone Wharf (area 3). The excavations at the two shafts (areas 1 and 2) were located within the heart of Mare's yard of the 1850s (Chapter 3.2), while the trenches at Instone Wharf spanned a large area in the south of the yard that was developed in the 1860s (Chapter 3.3).

The archaeological excavations were conducted according to the principles defined in the Museum of London's *Archaeological site manual*[1] and in accordance with the Museum of London's *A research framework for London archaeology*.[2] All archaeological features and deposits were fully surveyed. This enabled the information generated to be compared to historic maps and analysed alongside findings from textual documentary research. The result has been that we can now identify the development of the ironworks with date ranges for the construction of many of the yard's buildings and structures, and can place the archaeological findings within the larger context of the ironworks as a whole.

Among the maps that were located over the course of archaeological work was a survey plan made of the yard for its sale by auction in 1913 (Fig 39), which came to light following an advertisement by Crossrail for any information that the public might hold on the ironworks. The map was kindly donated by Charles Warner and has since been referred to as the 'Charles Warner map'. The map is an invaluable source of information for interpreting the archaeological evidence found. It covers the whole of the yard and details the function of each building and shed at the time of the closure of the Thames Iron Works. While building uses did change over time, the labels provide a useful starting point for the identification of many of the structures on site. A further map detailing the layout of the yard and labelling the various buildings and structures was subsequently found in a contemporary publication, *Engineer*, which frequently included material concerning the ironworks and in December 1895 ran a several-page article (Fig 37).[3] Comparison of these two maps alone began to show the changes that had occurred in the last two decades of the yard, including the redevelopment of the north slip as a boatbuilding shed, the transformation of a part of the largely defunct steam hammer workshops

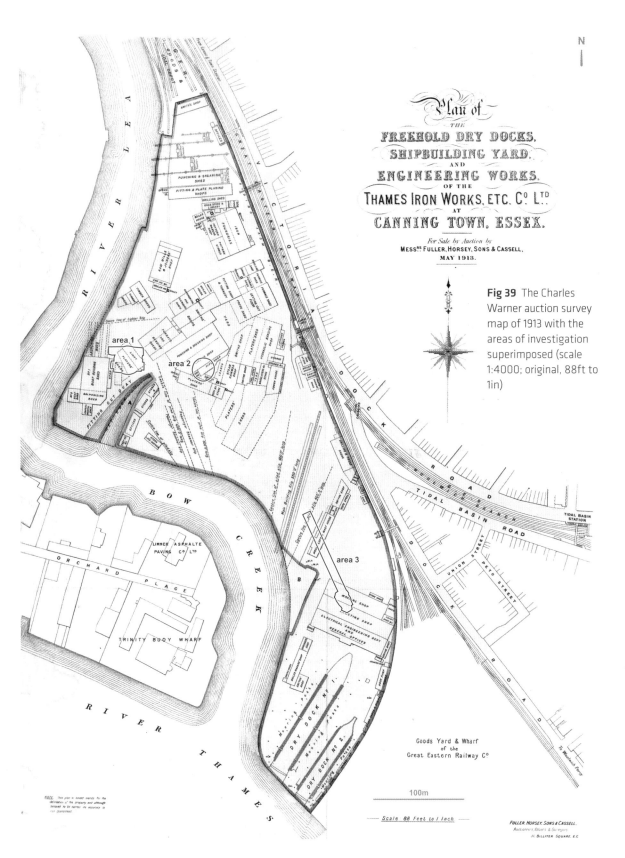

Fig 39 The Charles Warner auction survey map of 1913 with the areas of investigation superimposed (scale 1:4000; original, 88ft to 1in)

into an electricity generating station and the altered use of the showcase engineering building fronting the Thames (Fig 29).

It was not possible to work out the chronological sequence of the structures found from their building materials alone. The bricks used were of types readily available in the London area for the entire life of the yard, generally yellow stocks which probably derived from brickyards along the Thames estuary in north Kent or south Essex and dark red bricks from brickyards in the London area. The maps, however, enable us to form some idea of what the various areas were used for and how the yard developed over time.

The ground surface was apparently created by laying down large quantities of clay and alluvium (marshy silt probably excavated from elsewhere in the yard or close by), which was then covered by a metre-thick layer of industrial ash and clinker. This arrangement was seen at each investigation and formed the ground surface for the entire Thames Iron Works. The upper layer may have been derived from industrial waste, of which there was a ready supply from local iron production and coke burning. The material seems to have been available for the duration of the development of the yard, as it forms a consolidated ground surface in the areas developed in the late 1840s or early 1850s and in the south portion of the yard developed well into the 1860s. It could have come from a single source, as the same material, or very similar, was seen everywhere, possibly supplied as waste by the coke burners which previously occupied the site. However, the operation would need to have been on a huge scale to provide the amount of material required and it is more likely to have come from several sources producing similar material.

4.1 1860s development of furnaces and light platers' sheds (area 1)

Structures from two sheds were discovered in area 1, the earliest of which was a large rectangular building, aligned north-west–south-east, visible on maps from 1862 onwards (Fig 40). The 1867 OS map shows the building as having a solid west side and an open east edge. However, it was likely to have been a shed/building of light foundations as no traces of the walls were seen in excavation. Within the footprint of the rectangular building, several timber ground beams (S17, S21 and S23), possible floor joists, were seen and a fragment of floor planking survived. There were also four areas of concrete (S22 and S27) with lengths of timber insets and scars from further timbers. These are almost certainly bases for machinery, probably of a fairly light nature, secured by bolts going through the machinery into the wooden insets. Signs of the bolts holding machinery in place could be seen in the tops of the timbers.

The 1894 OS map shows further structures abutting the east side of the shed/building. These were two juxtaposed large brick structures: the larger a

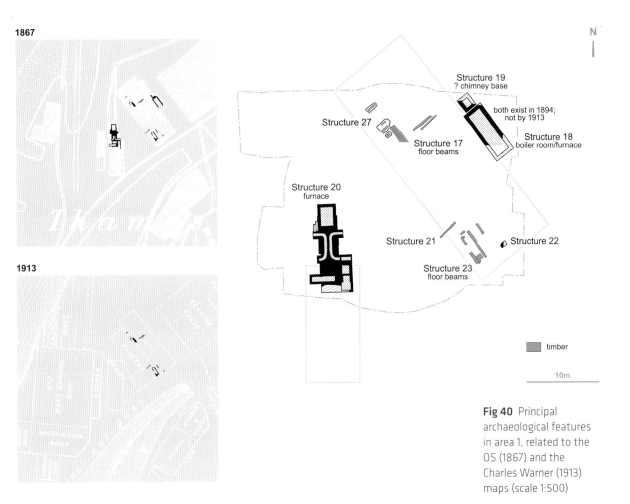

1867

1913

Structure 19
? chimney base

both exist in 1894;
not by 1913

Structure 27

Structure 17
floor beams

Structure 18
boiler room/furnace

Structure 20
furnace

Structure 21

Structure 22

Structure 23
floor beams

timber

10m

Fig 40 Principal archaeological features in area 1, related to the OS (1867) and the Charles Warner (1913) maps (scale 1:500)

boiler room/furnace (S18) and the smaller a possible chimney base (S19; Fig 40). These are visible on the 1867 OS map (Fig 40, inset) and disappear between 1895 (map published in the *Engineer*; Fig 37) and 1913 (Charles Warner map; Fig 39; Fig 40, inset). Both the structures appear to have been subjected to high temperatures, especially Structure 19, constructed of yellow stock bricks three widths thick. The boiler room/furnace (S18) was built of a mixture of dark red and yellow stock bricks four widths thick and its internal space was lined with heat-resistant bricks. The floor was also of brick, two courses thick. A metal pipe was found along the west face of the structure and may have been associated with machinery, possibly carrying steam or water. Burning inside the ? chimney base (S19) suggests that it was connected to the larger boiler room/ furnace (S18) above the level of survival. The heat-resistant bricks or firebricks were capable of repeated heating and cooling, and, usefully, the lining could be replaced without having to completely rebuild the structure.

The second shed/building discovered at the west of area 1 contained the best-preserved structure seen on the site. This shed/building contained a very substantial furnace (S20; Fig 40), shown on the OS map of 1867 as partly protruding out of the north wall of this building/shed. It appears unchanged on the map published in the *Engineer* in 1895 (Fig 37). The shed itself that housed the furnace was not identified, but it was probably of a light construction.

It is not clear what type of furnace was uncovered, as much of the structure was gone, but it was possibly a form of reverbatory furnace, of which the yard had several for converting scrap into iron blooms for the hammers to work.[4] It is not clear how the various elements of the furnace worked but it seems the lower working area to the south served a raised floor/hearth area in the middle of the structure, which was heavily charred (Fig 41). The floor structure was built over two parallel barrel-vaulted brick flues, which also showed evidence of exposure to extreme heat, and which were partially filled with accumulated cinders. To cope with the heat, the flues were lined with firebricks on which the maker's stamp 'POTTER' helps to date the furnace to after 1860.

'POTTER'-stamped firebricks were seen at a number of locations on site. These bricks were almost certainly made by James Potter at his brick and fireclay works in Scotland. They may have been made at a works built on the south side of Lock 5 on the Forth and Clyde Canal and taken over by James

Fig 41 The north half of the furnace (S20), view looking north; clearly visible are the flues and the portion of floor remaining above, possibly a hearth; the brick internal space, possibly an ash box, is at the top of the photograph

Potter of Glenfuir, Falkirk (Stirlingshire) by 1860. James Potter and Company was established by 1886. The brick and fireclay works moved to Glen Village, to the south of Falkirk, in the 1880s and became part of the Callendar Coal Company.[5] James Potter died 6 May 1890, aged 75;[6] the 'POTTER'-stamped firebricks, therefore, probably date from somewhere between the 1860s and the 1880s.

The flues of the furnace (S20) appeared to terminate at their north ends and may have become vertical at these points. The curving south-west arm of the flue seems to have terminated in the same way, but the south-east arm extended into a small brick-floored rectangular structure (Fig 40). The terminations of the flues appear to be reflected in the OS map of 1867 with tiny stubs protruding from the side. These were perhaps two small chimneys and might imply that exhausted hot air was sucked down from the raised firebrick floor area, through the south flue terminations and fed under the firebrick floor before being expelled from the chimneys via the north flue terminations. This would recycle the heat into the structure and cool down the exhaust slightly before it went up the chimney(s). The chimneys may have had adjustable dampers at their tops to regulate the heat inside the raised hearth area.

South of the flues, the brick-floored working surface (Fig 42) was edged with square firebricks stamped 'COWEN' and four slightly sunken areas. It is not clear how these sunken areas corresponded to each other or what they would have been used for. The 'COWEN'-stamped firebricks were made by Joseph Cowen and Company of Blaydon-on-Tyne, Newcastle (Northumberland), which was in operation between c 1823 and 1904, and have also been found on other London sites.[7]

Fig 42 The south part of the furnace (S20), view looking north-east, showing brick floor south of the flues

North of the flues, there was another unconnected brick-floored space (Fig 43). The floor and walls were not firebrick and had been badly damaged nearer the flues – no doubt due to constant heating and cooling. On the top of the masonry surrounding the sunken area were iron sheets attached to the tops of the walls. The metal sheets may have separated a portion of non-firebricks lower down from a section of firebricks above them, as a few firebricks survived above. The source of the heat for the furnace is not known and it seems unlikely to be the north structure directly, as it had not been lined with firebricks. Tramlines are visible on the OS map of 1867 leading directly to it (Fig 40), so if not a chimney (unlikely as the flues do not connect to it), it was a possible ash-collecting box below the heat source. The tramline would then have brought coal in and taken ash away from the same point.

If the furnace was for producing iron blooms, it seems likely that it was for purposes nearby, as the iron would cool quickly, though could have been reheated. The blooms produced from scrap were often passed through rollers or hammered before being cut into faggots and heated again, sometimes several times, thus ensuring uniformity of structure and composition, and purity.

The furnace may have been used in the forging of fittings, or possibly supplied the platers in the nearby shed with material to press plates independently of the large press sheds. The furnace may alternatively merely have been used as a reheater, to make iron malleable enough to be worked to 'shape plates and bend ribs to awkward shapes'.[8]

By the time of the Charles Warner map of 1913 (Fig 40, inset), the large rectangular building had either been replaced or incorporated into a group of new open-sided sheds to the west – the new 'light platers' sheds. The shed/building that housed the furnace appears to have been replaced by a larger

Fig 43 The north end of the furnace (S20), looking south-east; the brick-floored internal space (left, foreground) is possibly an ash box

shed and the furnace demolished or incorporated into a new building in the interim. This seems to have coincided with the redevelopment of the slipway to the immediate west as an area for the new boatbuilding sheds, which probably took place in 1895 or 1896 when the ironworks started producing lifeboats (Chapter 3.3). The light platers would have produced thinner plates for building iron hulls and possibly superstructures.

4.2 1850s–60s development of the engineers'/fitting shop (B6), engine house (B7), press/platers' shed (B8) and pipe shop (S16) (area 2)

Area 2 was centred on one of the oldest parts of Mare's Essex yard. Five separate industrial buildings or structures were identified. The defining features of this part of the site were two buildings (Fig 44), which probably date to the time of Mare's initial development of the site in the 1850s (Chapter 3.2). Buildings 6 and 8 are clearly identifiable on the 1862 embankment permission map[9] and

Fig 44 Principal archaeological features in area 2, related to the Charles Warner map (1913) (scale 1:500)

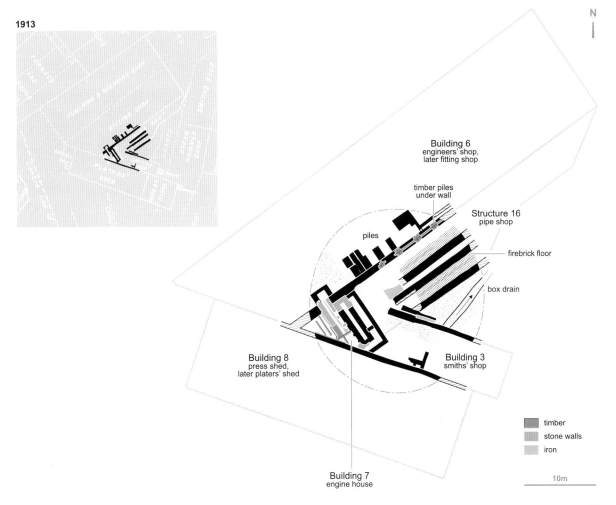

1913

N

Building 6
engineers' shop,
later fitting shop

timber piles
under wall

Structure 16
pipe shop

piles

firebrick floor

box drain

Building 8
press shed,
later platers' shed

Building 3
smiths' shop

timber
stone walls
iron

10m

Building 7
engine house

are labelled on the 1895 map published in the *Engineer* (Fig 37)[10] as being an engineers' shop (B6) and a press shed (B8) (Fig 45), creating an angle around which all subsequent buildings and structures were added. While the industrial processes that took place in the yard no doubt evolved over time to match changing manufacturing requirements and as new technologies were introduced, the same or similar processes seem to have taken place in the buildings of area 2 for their duration. Later, Building 6 would become the fitting shop and Building 8 one of the light platers' sheds, as shown on the Charles Warner map of 1913 (Fig 39).

The south wall of the engineers' shop (B6), in particular, demonstrated Mare's efforts to combat the soft ground on which the buildings were constructed. The wall was built on arched foundations (visible in the wall across the middle of Fig 45), which in turn were positioned over grouped sets of four pine (*Pinus* sp) timber piles driven more than 5m down into the gravels below the marshy silts (Fig 44). In addition, timber ties extended between the piles to stop the arches from spreading. These piles were tipped with heavy iron points to aid their penetration of the gravels below.

No internal structures survived from the press shed (B8; Fig 44). However, in the engineers' shop (B6) a number of machine bases were identified. The earlier of these bases were of brick and replaced over time with concrete bases, as

Fig 45 Area 2, with the floor of the engineers' shop (B6) in the foreground and the engine house (B7) behind, right, looking south-east

THE THAMES IRON WORKS 1837–1912

additional machinery was added and outdated machinery removed. By 1867 this building was served by an internal tramway visible on the 1867 OS map coming into the building from the east side (Fig 27).

The 1867 OS map also shows that by this date the outlines of an engine house (B7) and smiths' shop (B3) have been added (Fig 19; Fig 44). The engine house (B7) seems to have powered processes taking place in the engineers' shop (B6) via a gap in the wall. Fig 44 shows the complexity of the internal layout of the engine house (B7), which presumably housed a boiler and a means of distributing the steam power produced. Part of the internal construction was brickwork, with the areas of structure near the gap in the wall of the engineers' shop built in stone (Fig 44), no doubt to provide extra strength for fittings subject to high stresses. The part of the engine house (B7) which extended north-west into the engineers' shop (B6) was partially lined with voussoir-shaped 'COWEN'-stamped firebricks.[11] The inside of the easternmost wall was also of firebrick, which suggests that the heavy rectangular structure in the middle of the space held a boiler. The timber elements were probably floor joists and held a portion of surviving timber floor. It is not clear how access was gained, although the door may have been just to the west, along the wall of the engineers' shop (B6), with access from there.

In January 1895, Mackrow describes developments in the shipbuilding department of which this area formed the heart. He writes that 'a central station is being arranged whereby the engineers' fitting shop, smiths' shop, platers' shops, ship fitters' shop and the saw mills will all be worked by one set of boilers, as against three sets at present in use'. The old boilers were to be exchanged for 'modern Galloway boilers'.[12] As the engine house (B7; Fig 44; Fig 46) is at the centre of these buildings, it may have been their sole source of power, although it does seem fairly small for this and it is some distance from the smiths' shop (B3; Fig 44). If hydraulic power was used, no trace of it survives.

Fig 46 The engine house (B7), view looking south-east

The smiths' shop mentioned relates to Building 3 (Fig 44). One relatively uninformative stub of brick masonry survived within the smiths' shop, as well as two patches of a rammed surface made from the compaction of the ashy clinker forming the ground surface. Few traces of flooring survived anywhere on site, with most of the surviving surfaces being exposed rammed clinker dust. No doubt in some areas, particularly some of the shops where there was heavy machinery, flagstones, concrete or timbers had formed the floor.

Fig 47 View of area 2 looking south, showing the pipe shop (S16), to the left, with its two long firebrick-lined structures, and the engineers' shop (B6), to the right

Fig 48 The structures in the pipe shop (S16), view looking south-west

The smiths' shop (B3; Fig 44; Fig 47) was probably a roofed brick building, although it appeared to have an opening through to the pipe shop (S16), which may be the slightly separate rectangular open-sided shed marked on the 1867 and 1894 OS maps and the map published 1895 in the *Engineer* (Fig 37). The 1913 Charles Warner map (Fig 39) shows the pipe shop (S16) connected to the engine house (B7) and smiths' shop (B3); the roof was possibly extended. The Charles Warner map is the only one to name the pipe shop (S16), which contains two structures possibly used for ironworking, lined with 'POTTER'-stamped firebricks (above, 4.1) and each bisected longitudinally by a single skin of 'POTTER'-stamped brick partitions (Fig 48). The structures may have been directly related to metalworking and the production or alteration of pipes or may have carried hot waste gas and acted as flues taking hot gas away from the engine house or another furnace nearby. A wall that would have enclosed the firebrick-lined structure closest to the fitting had been demolished and removed entirely.

The area to the south-east of the pipe shop was an open space, marked by more patches of the rammed clinker surface. It contained a brick-built box drain with an iron cover (Fig 44), which was probably fed by drainpipes running down the north wall of the smiths' shop (B3).

4.3 1862 development at Instone Wharf (area 3)

Development south of Charles Mare's old yard began *c* 1862 with the acquiring of land that stretched as far as the south-east edge of the mast house and mould loft (B4) (Chapter 3.3; Fig 19; Fig 49). To the west of Building 4, the area for the three new slipways must initially have involved some form of ground preparation including the removal of the embankment that protected the area from flooding by the Lea. The embankment may have been left in place while the upper portion of the slipway beyond the trench was constructed and the ground raised. The old mould loft burned down in 1861[13] (Chapter 3.3) and it seems likely that the replacement was fitted into the planned new development at the same time as the slipways and the south end of the new river wall were constructed (cf Fig 27).

Three separate elements from the 1862 development were seen in the north end of excavation at Instone Wharf: the southernmost timber-piled slipway (S8), the mast house and mould loft (B4) and the diverted river wall (S11; Fig 49; Fig 50). Separating the higher ground, on which Building 4 stood, from the lower ground of the slipway, the contemporary diverted river wall (S11) ran alongside the slipway as far as the north-east end of the mast house and mould loft (B4). It may have continued as an embankment after this point, although none is shown on either the map published in 1895 in the *Engineer* or the Charles Warner map of 1913 (Fig 37; Fig 39; Fig 51; Fig 52).

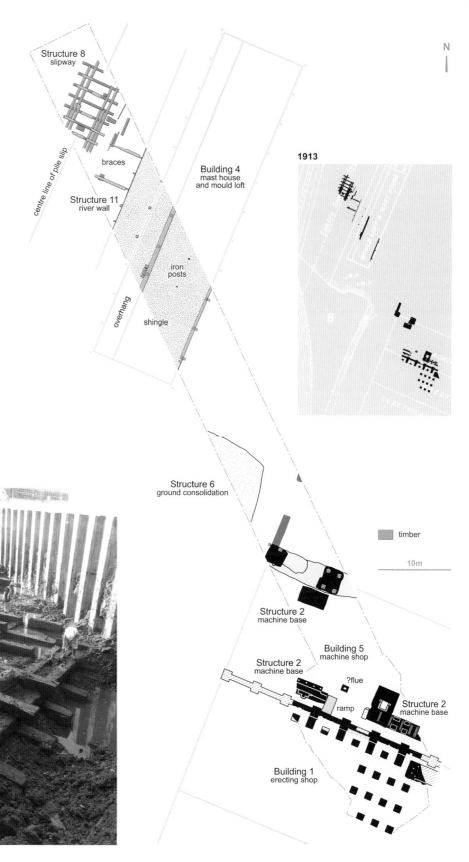

Fig 49 Principal archaeological features in area 3, related to the Charles Warner map (1913) (scale 1:500)

Structure 8
slipway

centre line of pile slip

braces

Structure 11
river wall

overhang

Building 4
mast house
and mould loft

iron
posts

shingle

1913

Fig 50 Area 3 at Instone Wharf, view looking south-east of the slipway (S8), in the foreground, followed by the river wall (S11) and mast house and mould loft (B4) in the background

Structure 6
ground consolidation

timber

10m

Structure 2
machine base

Building 5
machine shop

Structure 2
machine base

?flue

ramp

Structure 2
machine base

Building 1
erecting shop

Fig 51 The site at Instone Wharf during the excavation, view looking south-east from just upstream on the River Lea

machine shop
mast house
engineering building
erecting shop

Fig 52 A similar view to Fig 51, looking south-east, in 1906; the three buildings discovered are labelled along with the southerly portion of the showcase engineering building, which contained the general offices and fronted on to the River Thames
(National Maritime Museum, Greenwich, London, N23136)

Mackrow states that before the piling for the slipway commenced, it was imperative that the new protection be in place in accordance with the demands of the Marsh Authorities.[14] This probably entailed the construction of embankments to the north prior to the excavation of the ground for the slipways. The archaeological investigation suggests that the preparation of the ground for the river wall and mast house and mould loft probably took place contemporaneously, and then the slipway was excavated. Provided the area to the north had already been protected this would pose no problem. It seems likely that the whole south-west end of the mast house and mould loft and the area directly to the west of that was excavated to a certain depth and then gravel dumped to provide a consolidated working surface. The ground below the slipway (S8) and extending as far as the east edge of the mast house and mould loft (B4) was seen to consist of a very silty shingle. Construction of the new river wall (S11) is assumed to have occurred first, followed by construction of the mast house and mould loft (B4) and the slipway (S8). It is not known whether a cofferdam was erected between the river and the area being constructed prior to work beginning on the development, but there must have been some form of protection.

The river wall (S11)

The river wall (S11) took the form of a timber revetment consisting of horizontal planking attached to the landward side of timber piles (Fig 49; Fig 53). Alluvium was dumped behind the planking on the landward side and this was capped with the ubiquitous clinker. On the open side facing the slipway (S8), horizontal braces were positioned perpendicular to the river revetment. These were tied to the piles fronting the revetment by iron staples over 0.3m long which extended into the ends of the braces and held them flush against the revetment piles (Fig 54). At the other end of the braces, they were supported by vertical driven piles, strengthened on each side with an iron bracket which was probably bolted into the end of the brace, although the bolts had corroded

Fig 53 The river wall (S11), view looking south-east with the mast house and mould loft (B4) in the background; timbers shown bottom left probably provided bases for the shoring up of hulls on the slipway to the west (left); recently discovered finds, including a length of iron chain, <18>, can be seen on the left

away. The north-west ends of the braces also rested on unattached timbers that presumably supported them during their erection. It appeared that alluvium then was heaped against the new wall to help to secure it and to support the horizontal braces. Fig 53 shows the alluvium removed and the structure exposed. The timber piles, visible against the revetment, were more substantial originally but had heavily rotted. All parts of the revetment appeared to be softwood.

Fig 54 The junction of a horizontal brace with one of the piles retaining the planking, showing the large iron staples that held the two together, looking south-east

The mast house and mould loft (B4)

A photograph of the new dual-purpose building in 1863 shows two entrances (Fig 55). One entrance presumably went upstairs to the mould loft and one led into the mast house at ground level. The overhang on the left side of the building, mentioned by Mackrow (Chapter 3.3), is clearly visible (Fig 4; Fig 49). Wooden masts were probably stored at ground level. No trace of the

Fig 55 The mast house newly built *c* 1863, view looking north-east; the name would be changed to include the dry docks after 1864 or 1865; the man in the foreground may have been the master of the building (he may also appear in a later photo of 1866 (Fig 62) in the same working waistcoat)
(HMS *Warrior* Preservation Trust)

building above ground survived. However, there was evidence for a subterranean tank beneath it that would have contained water and may have been used as a mast pond for seasoning wooden masts in water. Shipyards where wooden boats were constructed often had mast ponds for this purpose, sometimes with access to a river or canal for floating the masts in or out. The tank consisted of two revetments of differing construction and a mast pond area in-between which had later been backfilled – probably following the yard closure and demolition of the above-ground structure. The ground consisted of a surface of shingle (Fig 49; Fig 56). The mould loft was where the timber templates for the component parts of the ship's hull were made. The drawing would be replicated at a large scale or even life-size on the floor and then a wooden template produced from which the iron components could then be made elsewhere (Fig 57).[15]

The south-east edge of Building 4 appeared to have been created by cutting into the alluvial deposits and then building a revetment slightly in front of

Fig 56 The two revetments of the mast house and mould loft (B4) subterranean pond, with the line of piles driven in between it and the river wall (S11) in the foreground, looking south-east; the previously excavated area in the distance is being prepared for the concrete to be poured to form the floor of the Crossrail tunnel spoil storage facility

this (Fig 49); the excavated alluvium was then dumped behind it. The cut was not visible except where occasional wood shavings were present in the material to *c* 1m behind the south-east revetment, possibly representing the excavated edge. As with Structure 11 (above) the area was then raised to ground level with a dump of clinker. The excavation for the mast house and mould loft (B4) may have occurred at the same time as that for the river wall (S11). This would make sense as the alternative would involve cutting down to build the river wall and then re-excavating further along to build the mast house (and in effect potentially destabilising the new river wall).

Fig 57 A skilled loftsman at Vickers, one of Thames Iron Works's main rivals, works with a pattern
(The Dock Museum, Barrow-in-Furness. cat no. 6193)

Unusually, the south-east revetment was constructed with sets of two pine (*Pinus* sp) piles driven perpendicular to the revetment and the planking placed between them (Fig 49; Fig 58). In front of the planking, large timbers were positioned to be used as baseplates. These had regularly spaced mortice slots in the top, into which timber had been placed to further brace the planking (Fig 59). Each of these baseplates was made from a different wood – of oak (*Quercus* sp), elm (*Ulmus* sp) and pine respectively, from north-east to south-west – and it seems likely that they were all reused. The oak timber had signs of modification from a previous use, with holes running through it horizontally from a recess. The recess had been blocked up with a thin wooden cover which had been attached over the old holes (Fig 60).

Fig 58 The south-east revetment of the mast house and mould loft (B4) pond, looking south-east

Fig 59 (above left)
Detail of south end of the south-east revetment showing the baseplate with a wedge in one of the mortice holes, looking south-east

Fig 60 (above right)
Detail of north end of the south-east revetment showing partially broken cover over two holes from a previous use of the timber, looking south-east

The north-west revetment (Fig 49; Fig 56) appeared to have been constructed in an open area. In this case the pine piles used were single, but otherwise identical to those in the south-east revetment, *c* 0.30m square in section. To either side of the piles were pine baseplates; the planking presumably ran between them though none survived. During excavation of the inside of the mast house pond, traces of timber were seen higher up marking the edge of the mast tank infill, probably the planking extending up to ground level. The baseplates were bolted to each of the piles with sets of four substantial iron pins, two on either side extending from the outside of the baseplate right into the pile. The baseplates sat on groups of flat timbers *c* 0.1m thick; the structure may have rested on these while it was being constructed. The piles in both revetments presumably extended up above ground level to form part of the above-ground structure of the building. Unlike the often iron-tipped, pointed piles seen everywhere else in the yard (which penetrated as much as 6m below the contemporary ground surface with their tips puncturing the gravels underlying the alluvial mud), the piles used in the mast house revetments were flat-bottomed and extended less than 1m below the shingle ground at the base of the pond.

Between the two revetments, a parallel line of metal upright posts, about 150mm diameter in section, were embedded in concrete in the shingle. They may have supported a floor above the pond. A further line of pine piles (Fig 49; Fig 56) to the north of the north-west revetment and equidistant between it and the river wall (S11) probably carried on upwards above ground level to support some form of outer wall for the mast house and mould loft (B4), which appears on the Charles Warner map to have a section that did not overhang but extended out at ground level (Fig 39). The section to the north of this may have had an overhang, but it also appears to have had a solid wall continuing, possibly also supported by these piles.

The south slipway (S8)

After the development of 1862/3 (Chapter 3.3), the Thames Iron Works had eight building slipways on the east bank of Bow Creek of lengths varying from 200ft to 400ft (60.96–121.90m). With the size of the ships increasing, the old upper slipways were no longer suitable for the largest vessels, the length of run to the bank opposite the slipways being too short to bring the ships up in time. The new southern slipways were longer and positioned so that ships built on them would have as straight as possible a run into the creek mouth which is at a right angle to the Thames.

The excavations uncovered the remains of the southernmost slipway (S8; Fig 49; Fig 61). Fig 62 shows the arrangement of the mast house and mould loft, the river wall and the slipway, and shows a ship being built on the southernmost slipway, as does the surviving photograph from *c* 1863 (Fig 55). It is notable that in the short time since the construction of the mast house, the diagonal strut timbers carrying the overhang at the front of the building have been replaced with vertical ones (cf Fig 55). These must have rested on some form of post-pad foundation, probably either concrete or stone; none were seen so they were probably removed during demolition. A waistcoated man standing proudly next to the building in 1863 was possibly the master of the mast house; similarly waistcoated men appear in Fig 62 of 1866.

Fig 61 The southernmost slipway (S8) of the Thames Iron Works, view looking south-east (1.0m scale)

Fig 62 The Thames Iron
Works on 15 July 1866,
view looking north; the
slipway is clearly visible
between the large ship
being built (possibly the
Serapis) and the mast
house and mould loft;
at its rear end a partly
built scaffold suggests a
new vessel is under way
(Getty Images/Hulton Archive,
3090681)

Fig 63 shows the form that the excavated slipway (S8) took and the level of
survival. An account by Mackrow of how battleships were launched in 1901
explains how the slipway worked.[16] The slipway would have consisted of a
frame to hold a set of two standing ways or 'groundways'. These were timber
slip planes, like upturned skis, that the ship would (excepting disaster) glide
down when launched. The framing for the hull would be erected on the keel
blocks positioned between the two groundways and raised up slightly. Shoring
timbers were positioned to support the hull as it rose. These were placed
against the hull and secured at an angle to the ground outside the slipway,
stopping the vessel from toppling over (Fig 64). When it came time to launch,
four wooden carriages would be built (sometimes six for the biggest ships),
one on either side of the ship at the front and the back to form a cradle. They
were positioned on the groundways, which had been greased beforehand with
tallow (a rendered form of animal fat) and spread over with 'soft soap and
linseed oil'.[17] The portions of the carriages resting on the groundways were
called bilge ways. Gangs of about 200 shipwrights would, in unison at the
signal, wield 7lb (3.18kg) mauls (a type of sledgehammer) to hammer wedges

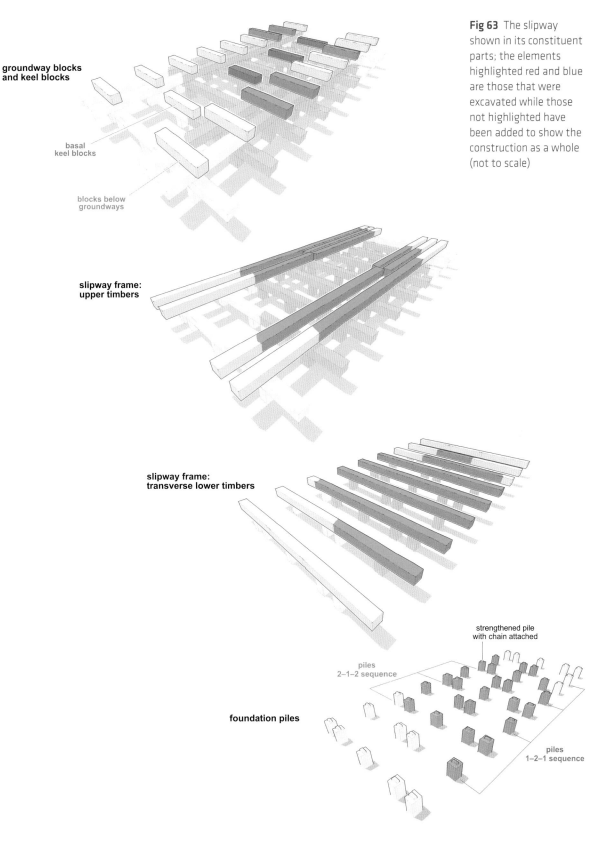

groundway blocks and keel blocks

basal keel blocks

blocks below groundways

Fig 63 The slipway shown in its constituent parts; the elements highlighted red and blue are those that were excavated while those not highlighted have been added to show the construction as a whole (not to scale)

slipway frame: upper timbers

slipway frame: transverse lower timbers

strengthened pile with chain attached

piles 2–1–2 sequence

foundation piles

piles 1–2–1 sequence

THE ARCHAEOLOGY OF THE THAMES IRON WORKS

or 'drivers' between the bilge ways and the upper portion of the carriages (Mackrow calls these 'poppets') to raise the carriages flush with the hull and raise the ship very slightly off its keel blocks.

With the ship resting on the carriages, the shoring around the ship would be removed and the keel blocks knocked out from below the ship (bar a few below the forefoot which were left in place until just before launching). Within the carriage were special chocks called 'dog shores' (normally painted blue). These were made of very tough wood – usually 'Sabicu' (*Lysiloma sabicu/ L latisiliquum*) or 'African oak' (*Oldfieldia africana*). They held the ship from moving forward. When time came, weights would swing down and knock these out, and a hydraulic ram at the bow of the ship (the rear of the launch) would push against the foremost bilge log or a special block to start the ship moving down under its own weight. This could be a matter of fractions of an inch at first, seconds passing, then inches, then foot after foot until the whole ship thundered down the slipway.

When the ship hit the water, it carried the carriages in with it. They were tied with further, less weighty, hemp hawsers to anchor points on land. As the ship continued forward the carriages would float to the side. Hawsers, 7in (0.18m) thick in 1901, also ran from the ship itself, from bollard points on board, through the hawser pipes at the front of the boat to anchor points on the shore. These would bring the ship up after launch, although they often snapped with the strain of doing so. After all this the ship should be silently drifting in the river and tugs would then pull it to

berth. Generally, launches at the yard ran smoothly (Fig 65), and great care was made in the calculations and timings to ensure that the vessel went into the water without mishap during high tide. Occasionally, however, they did not go as anticipated. One that took an unusual course was that of the launch of the wooden, armour-plated gun battery *Thunder* in 1855, which Mackrow recalls launched herself a few hours early 'one morning while all hands were at breakfast'.[18]

The timbers of the slipway (S8) were well preserved, with the structure which originally held the groundways surviving. The groundways themselves were probably removed towards the end of the life of the Thames Iron Works. The structure consisted of three main components: an upper structure of longitudinally arranged timbers (Fig 63; Fig 66), a lower structure of repeating frame elements running parallel to the river (Fig 63) which held the upper structure in place, and an array of pine (*Pinus* sp) piles on which these rested, driven into the underlying alluvial mud.

The two sets of longitudinally arranged timbers had a noticeable, though shallow incline of 1m in 13.8m (roughly 7.2°) down towards Bow Creek (the lowest portion of the Lea). The groundways would have rested on short lengths (blocks) of timber attached to this upper structure and raising them off the frame. Some of these remained attached to the longitudinal timbers (Fig 63; Fig 66). On larger, later slipways, these short timber blocks were often stacked two or more deep. However, the photo of 1866 (Fig 62) suggests that in the case of our slipway (S8), the groundways would have been placed directly on to single blocks. They were attached to the two sets of longitudinally inclined timbers ingeniously, with triangular recesses carved in the wood for large nails to be driven through their sides into the tops of the timbers below. This reduced weakening the timber on the top surface and also meant that the nails could be driven at an angle, further securing the timbers and, like a picture hook, preventing the timber from sliding sideways. It also reduced the amount of iron required for the fixings. An iron fixing through the top would have needed to be much longer and stouter, and a hole would have to have been drilled from the top down into the timber below.

Timber blocks were additionally seen attached to the transverse timbers of the frame, along the midline of the slipway. These would have formed the base of the stack of timbers on which the keel would have been built – the keel blocks (Fig 63; Fig 66). Fig 67 shows what is probably the main (central) lower slipway adjacent to Structure 8, with the groundways prepared and the keel blocks laid in preparation for the building of the *Shikishima* in 1897.[19]

The longitudinal timbers were affixed to the underlying frames where they crossed with long vertical nails driven from the tops of the long timbers into the middle of the lower framing timbers. Also, where the longitudinal timbers rested on the framing timbers, the undersides appeared to be slightly recessed forming a very shallow halving lap joint. However, it was suggested that this may have been caused by the sheer weight of the timbers pressing on each other for 140 years.

Fig 66 The south slipway (S8), looking north-east, showing the two sets of longitudinally arranged timbers with surviving transverse timbers above to hold the groundways and surviving keel blocks with their triangular recesses along the centre; the flat board near the foreground at the centre is one of several laid as duckboards (1.0m scale)

THE THAMES IRON WORKS 1837–1912

Fig 67 Slipway prepared for the building of the *Shikishima* in 1897 at the Thames Iron Works, view looking north-east (*TIWG*, no. 10, 1897, 66) (National Maritime Museum, Greenwich, London)

Fig 68 The tenons of the piles jutting up from below; the vertical edges on either side mark the imprint left in the surrounding mud by the removal of the transverse timber resting on those piles

Removal of the framing timbers revealed a distinct arrangement of piles (Fig 63). The piles were arranged in a repeating pattern of 1-2-1, 2-1-2, 1-2-1, to allow for an even distribution of weight to be transferred by the slipway from the ship. The removal of the timbers also revealed they were connected to the piles by mortice and tenon (Fig 68; Fig 69), further strengthening the slipway frame. The piles and the slipway were made of pine (*Pinus* sp). A number of timbers placed in amongst the slipway frame may have served as duckboards (Fig 66) and a line of degraded timbers parallel to the immediate east may have been positioned to accept the shoring timbers for the hull.

It is not certain when the slipway (S8) went out of use, although it may well have been partly derelict before the end of the life of the ironworks. Fig 70, a photograph of 1887 of HMS *Sans Pareil*, clearly shows a build-up of silt partially obscuring the slipway. Maps provide further evidence for disuse. The photograph of 1866 (Fig 62) shows the slipway in use, with the framing for a new vessel under construction on the slipway, next to a partially built ship – possibly the troop ship *Serapis*.[20] The OS map of 1867 shows a line from the internal tramway system serving each of the three slipways (Fig 71). By the 1894 OS map only the main slipway is shown of the southern three, and the tramways have been moved to occupy the positions of each of the other slipways alongside (Fig 71). It may have been that the ships launched from the main central southern slipway simply became too large to allow ships alongside (cf Fig 3, dating to 1895). Alternatively, the reduction in orders to the yard may have meant that these other slips remained dormant, waiting to hold new ships but were never reopened.

Fig 69 The mortice holes on the underside of the removed transverse timber, which is seen here lying on its side outside of the excavation with a machine excavator's bucket resting on it

Fig 70 HMS *Sans Pareil* on the central southern slipway in 1887, view looking north; the heavily silted over south slipway is visible to the right (National Maritime Museum, Greenwich, London, G05565)

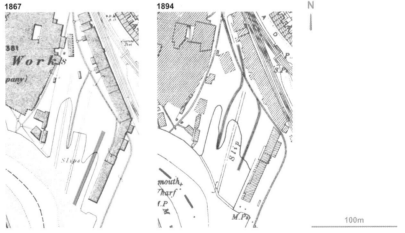

Fig 71 Detail of the portions of the 1867 and 1894 OS maps showing the absence of all but the main slipway by 1894; the internal tramway (blue) has been brought up on either side of the main slipway (yellow) in the location of the excavated slipway; the excavated slipway (S8) is highlighted in red (scale 1:4250)

On top of some of these riverine deposits, which contained a large amount of timber shavings, a fragment of the upturned flat bottom of a small rowing boat was discovered, probably reused as a duckboard (shown *in situ* on Fig 53, right). The boat's flat bottom was found to be made of oak planks with an added 'skeg' or fin of softwood (Fig 72). It is tempting to consider that the boat fragment may be part of one of those that was used to ferry workmen between the Middlesex and Essex banks of the yard (Fig 73) supplementary to the chain ferry.

THE THAMES IRON WORKS 1837–1912

Fig 72 The flat bottom and added skeg (at stern) of an unusual small rowing boat being recorded, looking north

Fig 73 A view looking east of the workmen disembarking for another day's work on the Essex bank of the yard, 1907–9
(MOL, image no. 004301)

Fig 74 Halfpenny <17> of 1862 showing Britannia on the reverse side (Diam *c* 26mm)

Observations of the riverbank parallel to the trench show an area which is slightly flatter and more evenly inclined than the bank directly upstream. While it may be a trick of the eye – or merely reflect the gradient of the bank where the slipways once came into the river – it indicates that there may be traces of the slipways still present below the silt on the waterfront.

Few finds were recovered. A halfpenny, <17>, of 1862 was discovered in the build-up of waterfront deposits in and around the slipway (S8) (Fig 74). Although the coin may have been dropped some time later than this, it is notable that it shares the same date as the slipway within which it was found.

One of the piles was strengthened with iron corner brackets (Fig 75; Fig 76) and had a chain still attached to it, similar to one found nearby (Fig 77, <18>). The chain may have been one of several anchor points for the hawsers to either bring up the boat or the carriage. If this is the case then the hawser would have been attached to the chain via a fitting which is now lost. The use of forged and fire-welded anchor chains was adopted by the Royal Navy in *c* 1809.[21] At first the links were of open form but in 1812 the stud link form with a central brace appeared and had become the main form by the mid 19th century, having the advantage of preventing the chain from knotting.[22] The chain found at the excavation appears to have the two types in an alternating sequence of two plain, six braced and seven plain links. The chain may well have come from Brown Lenox Company Limited, who founded their London factory a short distance away at Millwall in 1812 or 1813 and became the sole suppliers of anchor chain to the Admiralty from the mid 19th century

Fig 75 The slipway (S8) with the transverse timbers removed, looking south-east; a strengthened pile (highlighted) may have been an attachment point for one of the hawsers for bringing up the carriage

<18>

Fig 77 Length of chain <18> found in the silt, probably part of the chain found around the strengthened pile (link L *c* 210mm)

(although the chain produced for the Admiralty may have been created solely at their other factory in Ynysangharad, Pontypridd, Glamorgan).[23]

Only a few of the other metal fragments found were retained as most were so badly rusted they simply fell apart in the hand. One, <20>, was possibly a much corroded fragment of butt-strap for joining together two iron plates (Fig 15). The holes appear to follow a linear pattern, and are probably rivet holes arranged in double chain format. In 1869, Reed commented that 'The double chain-riveted butt-fastening … is now very extensively used in the construction of merchant vessels and has been adopted in some of the more recent ironclads of the Royal Navy'.[24] The thinnest used were generally ⅜ in (9.53mm).[25] Alternatively, the plate may have been one of those employed by rivet heaters to hold the rivets in the fire (Chapter 2.2; Fig 15).[26]

Several fragments of worked wood were retained, along with three leather boots. The boots were old and worn when discarded. Two had been cut up for reuse, but they too are dated to the 1860s (or slightly earlier) by their style and construction details. They have straight soles, square toes which are rounded off at the corners and high toe springs (all typical features of mid to late 19th-century boots[27]), with machine stitching (which was introduced in the shoe industry in 1842) and stacked leather heels, ranging in height from 1in to 1½in (25.4–38.1mm). They are practical working boots which, at 13s 6d a pair in the mid 19th century,[28] would have cost the best part of a week's wages for a labourer.

The largest (an adult size 11–12) is particularly sturdily made with a low 1in (25.4mm) heel, evidence for hobnails, thick internal linings and a straight-topped heel stiffener. The vamp is missing (cut away for reuse) but, like the two-piece back quarters, was made from cattle hide used flesh-side out (suede). The fact that the quarters are two-piece would suggest that this is a 'high-low' laced ankle boot of a type common in the late 18th and early 19th century rather than a similar but slightly later lower 'blucher' boot,[29] although its toe shape and high toe spring suggest a mid 19th-century date. Presumably high-lows, described as 'muddy high-lows' by Sam Weller in Dickens's *Pickwick papers* (1836),[30] were still made and worn alongside the more fashionable bluchers or it could simply have been a blucher boot made with two-piece quarters.

Another large men's boot (an adult size 10) is also lined but made from thinner leather much of which deteriorated in the ground. It is, however, identifiable as a blucher boot, with a high vamp and evidence for machine-stitched lapped quarters which would have laced over a missing tongue. The smallest boot (adult size 6) is a possible woman's boot, made from finer leather, possibly calf, with a higher 1½in (38.1mm) heel. Its vamp has also been cut away for reuse, but the linings and high quarters survive, stitched with fine machine stitching and reinforced internally with a textile tape or braid. The boot may have been given to one of the younger rivet gang boys at the yard by a female relative.

A note on the southern slipways and the *Thames Iron Works Gazette*

The *TIWG*, while of incalculable benefit to the study of the yard, was also written with political motive and can be misleading. An example of this is in the dating of the creation of the southern slipways. Initial research conducted into the date was confused by several sources which state that HMS *Warrior* was most likely built on the large central southern slipway. It is not always clear where this information comes from, but a potential source is Arnold Hills himself (Chapter 3.3). During an impassioned speech at the launch of HMS *Thunderer*, recounted in the *TIWG*,[31] Hills clearly states that the *Thunderer* was being launched from the same slip as HMS *Warrior*, half a century earlier. This, however, conflicts with several sources now identified and could not have been the case.

HMS *Thunderer* was certainly launched from the central southern slipway which had to be greatly strengthened and enlarged to deal with the sheer size of the super dreadnought. If HMS *Warrior* was launched from the same slipway, it would imply that the set of three southern slipways (or at least the central of the three) was constructed sometime in the 1850s (the *Warrior* being built from 1859 to 1860). A map of 1862, however, shows that these slipways had not been built at that time (Fig 19).[32] In confirmation of this, other sources point to HMS *Warrior* being launched from the old main slipway at the heart of Mare's yard and also that the southern slipways were most likely constructed *c* 1860–3, probably in 1862.

Firstly, there is sworn testimony from a lawsuit brought by tug operators, Messrs Watkins and Company, against the Thames Iron Works for damages caused during the launch of the *Cyclops* in 1871. During the response from the Thames Iron Works, several statements were made. These statements were that the slip from which the *Cyclops* was launched was the same one from which HMS *Warrior* had been launched, and that this slip was 800ft (243.80m) up from the Thames and angled at 45° down the creek. This would point to both ships being launched from the main upper slip.[33] Secondly, the image of HMS *Warrior* on the stocks (Fig 28) clearly shows two buildings in the immediate foreground to the right and one large one on the left. This view only makes sense if taken from a vantage point just west of the upper slips. Thirdly, Barry refers to the southern slips as 'the new slips'.[34] Lastly, Mackrow writes that there was a concern that HMS *Warrior* would not be brought up quickly enough after launch before hitting the opposing bank of the river. As a result, dozens of logs were placed in the water to act as buffers. The logs were placed by where, at the time of writing, the 'sheer legs' stood.[35] The angle necessary for the ship to hit the logs reveals it had to have been launched from the main northern slip. As it was, the ship did hit the logs, and several people who had clambered on to them to watch the launch received a dunking in the filthy river, though none were hurt.[36]

The yard was in dire straits at the time of the launch of HMS *Thunderer* in 1911, with the battleship the last order of any significance on the company books. One can hardly fault Arnold Hills for use of poetic licence to add a little drama to the occasion of the launch. For him, the launch was the culmination of years of effort expended to demonstrate that the ironworks could handle ships of the largest type and he was fighting to save his shipyard. Hills cared deeply about the yard itself and also that it continue to serve the local area as an employer.

The engineering building (B1) and machine shop (B5)

The south part of the archaeological excavation took place in the area that was extended into after 1864 (Fig 19; Chapter 3.3). The maps after this time show a space between the mast house and mould loft and the new buildings there, which included the showcase engineering building and the two dry docks between it and the Thames. The photograph of the dry docks being built in 1864 and 1865 (Fig 78)[37] show the dry docks well advanced with the engineering building not yet built at that time, although scaffolding in the background suggests that it was underway. Fig 79 shows the engineering building being built at its south-west end nearest Bow Creek. Fig 80 is a similar view of the site before development and shows the degree to which the ground had to be raised and the embankments rebuilt to create the quayside; the buildings in the background were associated with bringing coal ashore for the coke burners (Chapter 3.1).

The excavation area partly overlapped the footprint of the north half of the engineering building and straddled the machine shop shown on the Charles

Fig 78 The large (west) dry dock under construction *c* 1865, view looking north; the buildings along Victoria Dock Road are still visible in the background (*TIWG*, no. 7, 1896, 88)
(National Maritime Museum, Greenwich, London)

Fig 79 The engineering building under construction, view looking south (*TIWG*, no. 7, 1896, 86)
(National Maritime Museum, Greenwich, London)

Fig 80 The site of the dry dock and engineering building before development, view looking south (*TIWG*, no. 7, 1896, 94)
(National Maritime Museum, Greenwich, London)

THE THAMES IRON WORKS 1837–1912

Warner map of 1913 (Fig 49, and inset). The ground floor of the engineering building seems to have been arranged as two long interconnected rooms extending to double storey height, and with further offices, including the drawing office,[38] in rooms above the southern of the two large ground floor spaces. The two large rooms were each effectively contained within separate brick buildings, sharing a wall and with access to each other at ground floor level. The large ground floor space at the front facing the Thames was lit by big windows, with the rooms above lit by windows and glass roof lights. The northern of the two rooms seems to have been lit by window lights running the full length of the roof and does not seem to have had an upper storey above. It may have had windows similar to those facing the Thames at the front of the building, but no external views of the building from the north have been found. A photograph of 1867 (Fig 81) shows a view of the inside of one of these two large workshops, probably the north workshop which was excavated.

Fig 81 The inside of a large, very crowded engineering workshop, possibly the later erecting shop, in 1867; the large machine on the left is a slotting machine and the iron structure straddling the room just below the roof is a travelling crane which moved up and down the bay carrying heavy loads (Getty Images/Hulton Archive, 2638867)

Fig 82 View showing the large machine shop, probably the southern of the two large ground floor spaces of the engineering building (*Engineer* 1895, 575 fig 7)

Fig 83 The *City of Winchester* lifeboat launched in 1902, with the erecting shop's outer north wall on the right, view looking north-east; the machine shop is the shed building with the glass roof between the sails of the lifeboat and the mast house and mould loft is to the left
(Science Musuem Library/ Science & Society Picture Library, MS 616/1, 46)

The engineering building was originally used for marine engineering and included a vast array of heavy machinery for producing shafts, boilers and other machine parts for the ships. After the marine engineering arm moved to John Penn and Sons, the building was given over to the civil engineering department, as an addition to their premises at the north of the yard (Chapter 3.3). The map published in the *Engineer* (Fig 37) shows that the building at least was still used for shipbuilding purposes in 1895.

The machine shop (B5, Fig 49; Fig 83) was a shed built on to the north-east edge of the engineering building and appears to have been added between 1895 and 1902. It is not marked on the OS map surveyed *c* 1894, although an intriguing line of little rectangles parallel to the 'girder shop' (later the erecting shop) on the 1895 map in the *Engineer* (Fig 37) may represent the building being constructed. If that was the case, however, it is surprising that it does not get a mention in the *Engineer* article.[39] In 1902, the civil engineering department took over the machine shop shed and its machinery.[40] The historical catalogue describes the remainder of the south site as 'mainly devoted to the erection of large structures'.[41] The Charles Warner map of 1913 (Fig 39) labels the northern of the engineering building's two large rooms as an 'erecting shop', so presumably this meant the civil engineering department took over both the machine shop and the large north room of the engineering building at the time. The same map shows the southernmost room, formerly marine engineering, as electrical engineering, so it seems with the acquisition of John Penn and Sons around the turn of the century that the marine engineers left the site altogether (Chapter 3.3). The civil engineering department was also an innovator. One of its best exports in later years was the Hone patented grab excavator – a type of machinery now ubiquitous to building sites (Fig 84); George Hone was an employee of the yard whose revolutionary design became the template for later technology.

In preparation for the new buildings, the ground had been raised and consolidated in the manner customary at the yard. An area, Structure 6, between the mast house and mould loft (B4) and the new engineering building appears to have been further consolidated with heavy furnace waste material, possibly to fill in an old inlet of the creek. The embankment along the creek frontage was replaced and a quayside was built (later to become Instone Wharf). The degree of ground raising necessary can be seen in Fig 80 which shows the area prior to development.

Fig 85 shows the remains uncovered in the trench. The trench straddled both the machine shop (B5) shed and the erecting shop (B1), the buildings being

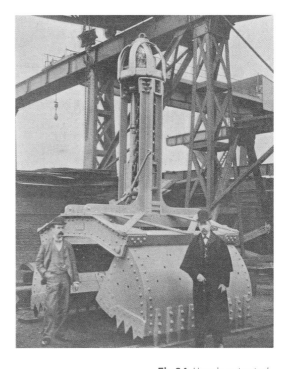

Fig 84 Hone's patented grab excavator, 1895 (*TIWG*, no. 2, 1895, 62) (National Maritime Museum, Greenwich, London)

Fig 85 The excavated area of the erecting shop (B1), on the right, and the machine shop (B5), left, separated by the main north-east wall of the engineering building, looking south-east

separated by the main north wall of the engineering building (Fig 49). The red brick wall was of a substantial construction with a stepped base built on deep continuous concrete foundations. The bricks from the main wall between the erecting shop (B1) and the machine shop (B5) were London-made dark red bricks. These have wide deep frogs with a small cross in the centre of the frog – some sort of distinguishing mark.

The line of the wall was further strengthened by brick piers (Fig 49). The arrangement of piers echoes the appearance of the frontage. However, since there is no known photo of the inside of the machine shop it cannot be confirmed whether the piers separated windows. The light presumably would have come into the shed and the erecting shop (B1) from the glass in the roof. Any possible lighting issues would cease to be a problem around the turn of the century, as large parts of the yard began to be electrically lit from the mid 1890s. By 1902 the engineering building, along with the machine shop (B5), was lit with bright arc lamps.[42] The workers would have greatly benefitted from the fact that their work could now be well lit any time, day or night.

An area in the middle of the wall appeared to have been an opening at ground floor level but had been bricked up. On both sides of the bricked-up opening, the piers were cornered with 'bullnose' bricks, so-called because of their slightly curved end. These yellow bullnose bricks were stamped 'B.B.C.W' in the shallow frog base. This is a rare mark in London and as yet there is no indication as to where these bricks were made.

The erecting shop (B1)

Within the erecting shop (B1) itself, little survived of the internal structure (Fig 49). The only remains encountered were a number of concrete bases aligned with the wall (Fig 86). Most of these formed an array of concrete foundation pads which may have held a flagstone or concrete floor or possibly a timber floor. Traces of wood near the wall and recesses in the brickwork do suggest a timber floor with floor joists extending perpendicular to the wall holding floor boards (Fig 87). This seems unlikely due to the sheer weight of machinery that the floor would have had to hold, but it is difficult to see what else the recesses were for.

Where the concrete pads coincided with the piers of the wall they were joined to

Fig 86 The east end of the erecting shop (B1), looking south-east; the large concrete bed in the background probably held very large machinery and was the only definite machine base in the room; the walls, to the right, belong to the foundations of a later building visible on maps from the 1950s; the concrete pad, in the foreground, abuts a pier and appears to have been partly gouged out, possibly to remove a machine base during demolition

THE THAMES IRON WORKS 1837–1912

Fig 87 The main wall of the engineering building showing recesses for possible timber floor joists within the erecting shop (B1), view looking north-east; the bricked up access is to the right, also showing the recesses (1.0m scale)

it and showed signs of possibly having held machinery. Each of the square foundation pads (Fig 49) was over 3m deep, which makes them seem more like concrete piles than simple floor pads. One surviving concrete machine base was seen at the far east of the excavation within the building. This was a very thick (0.7m) concrete block with the remains of iron fittings protruding up from the surface and was clearly intended to take a heavy machine. It is not possible to know with any certainty how the machinery was arranged in each of the buildings, nor what machines were positioned on specific concrete bases. The documentary sources, however, do list machinery employed at different times within the yard and give some idea of which buildings they were housed in. The historical catalogue lists machinery present in the civil engineering department in addition to that in the machine shop, which could have rested here – presses, croppers for angle iron, plate milling, hydraulic presses, a bending press and 'a complete equipment of lathes, slotting, planning and milling machines and drills'.[43] It seems more likely, however, that these machines were in the north civil engineering yard.

The machine shop (B5)

The probable remains of the north-east wall foundations of the machine shop (B5) were seen running parallel to the engineering building. The foundations consisted of a strip of deep, very loosely concreted sand and gravel interspersed with concrete bases 1–1.5m thick for iron stanchions. The concrete bases were set over groups of four timber piles, which extended below the depth of the excavation. Extending out perpendicular to the north-east wall foundation mentioned above, and cutting into it slightly, was a further foundation filled with a sandy yellow orange concrete (Fig 49). A photograph from the historical catalogue shows the machine shop clearly constructed of iron beams and metal sheet (Fig 88).[44]

The historical catalogue lists the machinery here as 'straightening rolls and press planning, punching, shearing and cropping machines, radial drills, cold saw, etc'.[45] It also describes how 'at the centre of the shop rails are laid for locomotive cranes and trollies of either 3ft [0.91m] or 4ft 8 and ½inch [1.43m] gauge'.[46] Machinery may have been replaced over time and it is unlikely that old concrete foundations would have been removed, so some of the bases may not correspond to the machinery described above. However, given that the building was fairly new, it seems likely that the machine bases uncovered in the machine shop (B5) do correspond to the machines on this list. The historical catalogue describes all the machinery in the machine shop as electrically driven.[47] This may have been the case in 1911, but was probably a recent development. The article in the *Engineer* states that the engineering building's shops were steam-powered by three high-pressure engines and one compound engine,[48] totalling 220 horsepower.[49] The power was presumably distributed around the engineering building and probably the machine shop via belts, shafts and wheels. The noise must have been deafening.

Fig 88 A three-ton locomotive steam crane at the entrance to the erecting shop, with the machine shop to the left, view looking north-east; faintly visible to the left of the crane is one of the turntables that allowed the vehicles using the internal tramlines to change tracks and direction in the yard, a portion of the tramline clearly curves round into the machine shop; the cranes were both at use in the yard and also for sale – being marketed for use with Hone's patented grabs
(Science Musuem Library/ Science & Society Picture Library, MS 616/1, 82)

In the machine shop (B5), the concrete bases were found for three or possibly four separate groups of machines, all grouped together as Structure 2 (Fig 49; Fig 89). They were arranged on either side of an empty area, which probably marks the position of the internal tramway lines mentioned above. At the north of the excavation a rectangular machine base of unknown purpose was seen by the wall. Against the south wall, two sets of concrete bases were seen. The north-westernmost of these took the form of a heavy concrete feature with a sunken central portion, rising at either end as if to accommodate a large wheel, possibly a flywheel. The stubs of four, 1in (25.4mm) thick iron attachment points protruded on the north side, while a recess containing rotten wood opened on to the sunken central portion.

The south-east concrete bases consisted of an area of concrete up to *c* 0.3m thick built up against a very heavy concrete base to the immediate north-west (Fig 49; Fig 90). This base consisted of a raft of concrete over 0.7m thick with an opening at its centre, to expose a set of timbers bolted together and with thick iron attachment points protruding up through them (Fig 91). These seem to have formed the base for an exceptionally heavy piece of machinery as they were revealed later to be the top of a stack of timbers all bolted together and encased in concrete, with deep piles at each corner extending beyond the base of the excavation (Fig 92). The possible wheel base and the concrete bases to the south-east may have all been related as they corresponded to a similar alignment, with the central lengthwise axis of the possible wheel base roughly corresponding with a line of scars for machine feet on the concrete bases to the south-east.

Fig 89 The machine shop (B5), with the possible wheel base in the foreground, looking south; the flue or drain opening can be seen centre left with the south-eastern concrete machine bases behind

Fig 90 The south-east concrete bases (S2) of the machine shop (B5), looking east

Fig 91 The centre of the large concrete pad in the south-east of the machine shop (B5), looking west; timbers forming the upper part of the concrete-encased stack can be seen at the top of the opening, with heavy iron lengths for attaching machinery protruding up through the stack

A concrete ramp had been built against the wall. An opening higher up the wall may have lowered on to the ramp but this could not be confirmed. An opening built of brick led down to a large earthenware pipe, possibly a flue or a water pipe, which at a right angle ran toward the wall (Fig 49; Fig 89). A firebrick found in the top course of the brick box leading down to the pipe is of a very rare type. It is stamped 'M.T & Co' in the top/bottom surface and is the first known to be found in London. The location of the brickworks is

Fig 92 The timbers lower down the stack in the centre of the large concrete pad, in the south-east of the machine shop (B5), exposed when the building's floor level was removed, looking east

currently unknown, but bricks stamped 'M.T & Co' have been reported from the gardens at Alcatraz prison in San Francisco bay[50] and from Santa Cruz,[51] both in California (USA). During the removal of the wall, the pipe was destroyed and it could not be ascertained what the pipe linked up with at its west end.

Notes to Chapter 4

1 Museum of London 1994
2 Museum of London 2002
3 *Engineer* 1894
4 D Cranstone, pers comm 2014
5 *Falkirk C T*
6 *Dawn's genealogy page [Potter family]*
7 Smith 2005, 33–4
8 M Tucker, pers comm 2011
9 TNA, BT 356/11536
10 *Engineer* 1894
11 Smith 2005, 34–6
12 *TIWG*, no. 1, 1895, 6

13 *TIWG*, no. 7, 1896, 93
14 Ibid
15 *Mould loft*
16 *TIWG*, no. 26, 1901, 58–61
17 Ibid
18 *TIWG*, no. 5, 1896, 2
19 *TIWG*, no. 10, 1897, 66
20 SM, MS 616/1, 23
21 Jobling 1993, 5, 136
22 Bradney Chain and Engineering Company 1987, 3, 6; Jobling 1993, 136
23 GA, GB 214 D179
24 Reed 1869, 205, fig 149
25 Ibid, 182
26 Ibid, 340

27 Swann 1982, 42
28 Ibid, 45
29 cf Mould 1997, 127
30 Dickens 2009
31 *TIWG*, no. 50, 1911, 22
32 TNA, BT 356/11536
33 *TIWG*, no. 14, 1898, 57
34 Barry 1863b, 67
35 *TIWG*, no. 6, 1896, 50
36 Ibid
37 Buxton 2004, 158
38 *Engineer* 1894, 572
39 Ibid
40 SM, MS 616/1, 93
41 Ibid
42 Ibid, 95
43 Ibid, 93 and 95

44 Ibid
45 Ibid, 93
46 Ibid
47 Ibid
48 In a compound (steam) engine the steam is expanded in more than one stage, first in a high-pressure cylinder and then in one or more low-pressure cylinders, as a means for recovering energy and making the engine more efficient.
49 *Engineer* 1894, 573
50 *Gardens of Alcatraz*
51 Piwarzyk 1996

CHAPTER 5

LABOUR RELATIONS, OPERA AND FOOTBALL CLUBS

The transition of shipbuilding from old wooden shipyards to iron (Chapter 2.1) was accompanied by significant changes in employment practices and workforce arrangements. Those employed from the 1840s and 1850s to work the new steam and iron building yards 'effectively formed a separate workforce, hired and fired on terms that had little relationship to the traditional conditions of employment within the yards'.[1] Thames Iron Works was organised on labour principles which had evolved in the industrial shops and factories where steam power and iron working had been developed. Workers were waged according to the amount of time they worked – the motto of the Thames Iron Works was 'no work, no pay'.[2]

This was a break from the old system of 'gang-contract' which had existed in London and continued to a certain extent in the wooden building yards at least up until the mid 19th century. The gang-contract system worked along a series of relationships between the masters and the shipwrights responsible for overseeing each build. The Thames, as the old established leader of wooden shipbuilding, had particularly developed traditions regarding the relationship between yard owners and workers, and in setting the rates of pay for specific work. These had been set out in 1825, following a strike brought about by the Shipwrights Provident Union of the Port of London formed in 1824, and did not change until the 1850s, with the dramatic increases seen during the Crimean conflict. However, they only specified the 'local norms'.[3] The actual work to produce the ship was priced by the 'leading hand', an experienced shipwright who represented the gang and agreed the amount with the master of the yard. The master would receive a commission of 10% on the work.[4] This arrangement favoured the workers, as weekly wages would be paid as advances against the work, which if finished early, would see the remaining balance delivered to them as a bonus. If the work went over budget, however, the workers would continue to receive weekly wages until the ship's completion.

No such arrangement existed in the industrially organised new yards. On the contrary, other than those managers who were retained on a more permanent basis by the works, workers were employed entirely at the discretion of the owners who exercised absolute control over their capital investment. When work was in the yard, the hours were long and workers toiled for six days a week behind the high walls that shielded the yard from the surrounding community. During times of dispute, the owners could very effectively deal with resistance by simply denying workers access. In areas like Canning Town, shutouts such as that effected for four or five months in 1851 following demands for better conditions from the newly formed Amalgamated Society of Engineers were devastating to the local populace.[5] Families were often entirely dependent on the income from the yards, and with no money coming in would suffer terribly. Dickens wrote in 1857 in *Household Words*, that 'Hallsville, called into existence some ten years since by the Messrs Mare and Company's ship-building yard … [was] half depopulated by the recent bankruptcy of that firm'.[6] With less money on the streets, shops and businesses would suffer also – in effect the owners of the larger yards could hold the area to ransom. The weather also could bring work at the yards to a standstill, such as during the winter of 1854/5 when the Thames and Lea froze. The winter of 1866/7, which followed a poor wet summer and a massive downturn of work, was hard on the Thames, and in particular on Canning Town.[7]

The population of the parish of West Ham alone had exploded with the coming of industry to the Lea, with numbers growing from 12,738 in 1841 to 62,919 by 1871 (a huge increase on the 38,331 living there in 1861).[8] The population almost doubled over each of the next two decades, with 128,953 recorded in the 1881 census, and 204,893 in 1891.[9] In 1901 the population grew to 267,191 (Fig 93).[10] A great many of these people were crammed into the areas alongside the industry of the Lea and the docks, in housing often overcrowded and poorly served by sanitation. Open sewers in West Ham still existed in 1890. Due in part to these sewers, the marshy area was a breeding ground for malaria late into the 19th century,[11] and the open sewers were themselves a disgrace, with toilets at the backs of houses opening directly into ditches which drained into the Lea. These regularly flooded back upstream to cover the area with the regurgitated sewage and added industrial effluent to the mix. 'No wonder that the stench of the marsh in Hallsville and Canning Town of nights is horrible'.[12] Charles Dickens, who wrote on the state of the area in the mid 1850s with his brother Alfred, saw children playing, 'beside

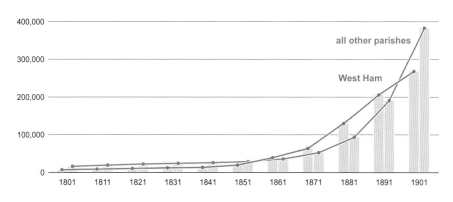

Fig 93 Census returns for the parish of West Ham compared to the total return for all the other parishes in the hundred of Becontree (the parishes of Barking, Dagenham, East Ham, Little Ilford, Low Leyton, Walthamstow, Wanstead and Woodford St Mary) (after *VCH* 1907, 345 [table])

another pestilential ditch … bubbling as if there were a miraculous draught of fishes just below … three ghostly little children, hung with their faces over it, breathing the poison of the bubbles as it rose, and fishing about with their hands in the filth for something'.[13]

Despite the formation of the Local Board of Health in 1856, following public pressure, the parish was not incorporated as a municipal borough until 1886 and missed out on many of the safeguards enjoyed by the London population since the Metropolitan Building Act of 1844[14] – such as the rights to freedom from poisoning with noxious industry. Also, the sanitation fell well behind the standards expected in London; an attempt to deal with sewage was aborted by the newly formed board in the 1850s.[15]

In the later part of the century, wealthier housing was constructed in the north half of the parish away from the industrial areas fronting the Thames and the Lea, and some attempts were made, often charitable, to replace slums with quality homes for the working class.[16] Much of the earlier building remained, however, often in the form of terraces of workers' cottages which were frequently squalid and ill-repaired. This was certainly true of parts of Canning Town, which had arisen along with Hallsville (which it later subsumed)[17] in some of the earlier development of the 1840s and 1850s. Writing of the housing in 1848, White commented on 200 new houses in Canning Town in his *History, gazetteer and directory of the county of Essex*, that they 'possess that grand desideratum for the working classes, the maximum of comfort with the minimum of expense'.[18]

Thames Iron Works in particular was affected by cyclical variations in the number of men it employed, as it increasingly moved towards building large warships and fewer merchant vessels. When the order came in for a ship, the flag high over the works was a signal for rejoicing in the neighbourhood, such as the case when HMS *Sans Pareil* was announced in 1885, 'and no wonder, when we remember that some £3000–5000 are paid in wages by the company weekly, most of which, if not indeed all, is spent in the district'.[19] The available data for the numbers of men and women employed at the ironworks is patchy – certainly in the pre-Arnold Hills era, but a general idea of scale of employment can be gauged from Table 2. The figures should be treated as general indications for employment and probably do not represent some of the more violent fluctuations that would have occurred. The pre-1870s figures are derived from secondary accounts and may represent capacity as much as actual employment. Those from the 1880s onwards probably more accurately reflect actual numbers employed but are yearly, so monthly fluctuations will have been smoothed out.

Table 2 Employment figures for Thames Iron Works with sources used

Year	No. employed	Source
1851	2000+	*The Times*, 27 August 1851, 5
1854	3000–4000	*ILN*, 28 October 1854, 409–10
1861	2500	*Mechanics' Mag* 1861, 95
1887	1529	Edward and Howarth 1907, 161
1892	2151	ibid
1897	2804	ibid
1902	3178	ibid
1907	1022	ibid

THE THAMES IRON WORKS 1837–1912

The working class were not left completely to the mercies of fortune. Beginning in the 1870s and 1880s, there was a strong drive to act against the recognised plight of those impoverished in the East End. Beatrice Webb, the socialist and later founder of the *New Statesman* magazine, assisted her cousin Charles Booth in his work surveying the slums of London, *Life and labour of the people in London* (1889 to 1903). She described the East End as the 'bottomless pit of decaying life'.[20] While charity did not directly address the underlying social and economic problems, much went the way of the East End, with the setting up of soup kitchens, shelters and other amenities for the poor, although the charity was often poorly coordinated and sometimes came with harsh conditions attached. An 1882 work of fiction by Walter Besant, *All sorts and conditions of men – an impossible story*, in which a man and wealthy woman venture to east London to create a cultural, educational and recreational institution[21] was a best-seller and bizarrely became a reality. With royal support and the money of a wealthy philanthropist, Barber Beaumont, the People's Palace was opened over the years 1888–92, at vast expense, for both the respectable entertainment and education of the working class of the East End. The educational part of the enterprise survives to this day as Queen Mary College, University of London, on Mile End Road.[22]

Arnold Hills (Fig 94) was the Oxford-educated son of the industrialist Frank Hills, who had acquired control of the Thames Iron Works in 1872 (Chapter 3.3). He was a naturally gifted athlete who excelled at several sports, eventually winning an international cap 'playing for the England football team that defeated Scotland 5-4 at Kennington Oval in 1879' and also becoming the English mile champion.[23] In 1880 he joined the board of Thames Iron Works.[24] His choice to live on East India Dock Road for five years among the community from which the yard drew its workforce says something of the social and political mindset of the man. At once he instituted educational and edifying activities for the local populace, intended to socially improve the area. However, there seems to have been a general reluctance or perhaps even disinterest among the local population – or at least, either long working hours or conversely unemployment made it difficult to devote time to these pursuits. Reminiscing on the time later, Hills wrote, 'it was like building ropes of sand – lectures, debates, concerts, gymnastics, temperance leagues, cricket clubs, football clubs … all passed through an ephemeral prosperity and then began to decline'.[25] The clubs were the beginning of more organised activities, which later included dedicated classes on science and mathematics for the workers and employees of the yard.[26] Hills was also involved in providing relief to the poor across London generally, becoming the chairman of the National Food Supply Association, which during the winter months supplied up to 5000 free daily meals for children from each of its several depots located throughout the burgeoning City.[27] Meals consisted of a pint of 'good hot soup, a slice of bread and a slice of bread cake'.[28]

Fig 94 Arnold Hills in the 1880s
(Wikipedia Commons)

Hills was a strange mix, with a strong desire to elevate, educate and ensure the health and happiness of the working class, while at the same time firmly expressing his dislike for union activity, or indeed any activity which challenged the relationship of employer to employee. In his own manner of peculiar paternalism he described such action – specifically strike action – as 'superfluity of naughtiness'.[29] He earned the howling disrespect of locals during his handling of the Great Dock Strike of 1889 (Fig 95). The boilermakers, labourers and joiners joined the strike and Hills brought 'black leg' labour across the picket line.[30] Further strikes in 1890 and 1891 were handled no better. Hills did not seem to have been aware of how badly this was perceived, or at least wished to negate or forget the fracture between men and management later when he wrote, 'For more than twelve months, after the great dock strike had set the torch to the powder-magazine of discontent, we had to fight whilst we worked … while our gates were picketed'.[31] He may have blamed the unions directly for the schism as opposed to the men themselves.

Hills took the view that the only way the Thames Iron Works would be able to compete with its northern contemporaries was by maintaining the quality of workmanship at the yard, and under conditions of the best (in his view) employer/employee relationship. 'The rights and interests of capital and labour when properly apprehended are co-ordinate … but let it always be remembered that the balance remains; there is no supremacy of labour in the eternal fitness of things, as there will be no tyranny of wealth in the ideal state'.[32] Beyond trying to mend fractured relations following the three strikes, Hills formed the *TIWG* as a line of communication between management and workers and to regularly put forward arguments for his version of best

Fig 95 The coal heavers' float at the London dock strike of 1889 (by permission of the People's History Museum)

THE THAMES IRON WORKS 1837–1912

employer practice. He also brought the educational, sporting, temperance and cultural societies under control of the works and reported them in the *TIWG*, although membership extended beyond the works itself. These were the 'Thames Iron Works Federated Clubs', operating from an office on Barking Road.[33] The most well known of these clubs still survives, with Thames Iron Works football club founded in 1895 (Fig 96) as part of the 'great social experiment' transitioning to professional play and becoming West Ham United in 1900.[34]

Fig 96 Thames Iron Works football club in 1896 with the West Ham charity cup; Arnold Hills is on the far left (*TIWG*, no. 7, 1896, 102) (Newham Heritage Service)

He clearly felt his relationship to his employees and to the business was almost of a father to his children, whose guidance alone might encourage them to turn their lives to fortune and prosperity. The poem (of which there was generally at least one in every issue of the *TIWG*) for May 1911[35] was 'If' by Rudyard Kipling (an acquaintance of Hills), with its final paternalistic line 'And – which is more – you'll be a man my son'. Reminiscing later, Hills wrote of his mindset in the early 1880s, 'The conquest seemed so easy, it needed only the directing will to evolve a new social era, to make an epoch in the annals of industrial employment to make every employee a friend, and every worker a sharer in the triumphant prosperity of the firm … To create a community of social interests, which should bind all the workers in this busy hive of industry in bonds of brotherhood not easily to be broken'.[36] Fig 97 shows the Thames Iron Works Operatic Society arrayed for a performance of *Pirates of Penzance c* 1896; the apathy of the Canning Town

Fig 97 Thames Iron Works Operatic Society dressed for a performance of *Pirates of Penzance c* 1896 (*TIWG*, no. 7, 1896, inside cover illustration facing p 83) (Newham Heritage Service)

locals to the efforts of the society seemed to particularly upset Hills who, in a rare slight, remarked on their failure to appreciate the points of opera as perhaps the result of 'not being sharp enough to understand them'.[37]

Despite the continuing difficulties faced by the yard, the Thames Iron Works under Arnold Hills was a forerunner among employers in its acknowledgement of workers' rights and, in addition to the 'good fellowship system', instituted such reforms as the 48-hour week,[38] with the eight-hour day introduced on the basis of nine hours wages in 1892 'long before other establishments were forced to do so'.[39] The 'good fellowship system' in some ways harked back to the gang-contract method of payment for those who participated. The system recognised the following: (1) 'that every workman shall be paid a recognized daily trade wage; (2) that all work shall, as far as possible, be given out at agreed piece-price; (3), that if the cost of production be less than the agreed price, that the difference shall be paid to those that have earned it, it [sic] exact proportion to the wages they have been severally paid'.[40] The scheme, when introduced, was wholly unpopular with the unions; perhaps it was seen as interfering with worker relations and the process of collective bargaining. Also, the setting of the appropriate piece-price was obviously wholly subject to decision by management and would have dictated the necessary work rate, with overtime an almost given. It was introduced during the height of the industrial actions of 1891 and 1892, evolving from a profit-sharing scheme tabled by Hills and rejected by the workforce.[41]

The works did also have a strong union presence, and views towards union activities seem to have softened over the years, with the *TIWG* running a whole series on the histories of the various unions represented in the yard;[42] indeed Hills acknowledged the effect of education granting voice to the East End, 'the new claims of enfranchisement and educated workers have naturally found their fullest, their freest, their most fiery discussion in the capital of the empire'.[43]

In addition to the good fellowship profit-sharing scheme offered by Hills, the works offered further incentives and safeguards to the employees and workers in the yard. The firm offered to pay one half of the insurance premiums of clerical and technical staff as part of its savings bank insurance scheme proposal[44] and also offered a pension investment fund.[45] Hills encouraged the shipyard workers to invest in the yard personally, with an issue of 5% redeemable debentures, available in units of £1 only.[46] They also set up an accident fund – up and running by 1895, with subscribers as of '12 December … 1003 men and 143 lads'.[47] Sadly there were often accidents at the yard, many of them minor, although sometimes fatal. Accidents were not limited to the workers. Even getting on to site could be dangerous. In 1912, Clement Mackrow – George Mackrow's son and shipbuilding manager after 1907 – was killed in an automobile crossing the railway into the ironworks (Fig 98).[48]

Fig 98 The White Gates level crossing across the rail line running parallel to Victoria Dock Road, one of the few entry points to the yard, in 1904, view looking south-west
(Newham Heritage Service)

Arnold Hills was not the first shipbuilder to address safety concerns in the East End, nor the first to put his own money into an institution to better the health or happiness of the yard workers. Recognising the lack of adequate medical provision in Blackwall, following the death of a shipyard worker at C J Mare and Company who might have lived had there been a hospital closer than the London Hospital in Mile End, Poplar Hospital for Accidents, the first casualty hospital for dockworkers, was opened in 1855 in the old East India Docks Custom House at the north-west corner of the dock (Fig 99).[49] The hospital was the initiative of Samuel Gurney, of Overend and Gurney, Money Wigram and others, including Charles Mare (Chapter 3).

Fig 99 Poplar Hospital, East India Road (*ILN*, 12 June 1858, 596)
(Look and Learn, U314008)

Notes to Chapter 5

1 Evans 2004, 11
2 Barry 1863a, 219
3 Arnold 2000, 19
4 Ibid
5 Ibid, 37, 52
6 Dickens 1857, 241
7 Ibid, 78–9
8 *VCH* 1907, 345
9 Ibid
10 Ibid
11 Clifford 2011, 115
12 Dickens 1857, 242, in Clifford 2011, 114

13 Ibid
14 Cherry et al 2005, 291
15 Powell and Sainsbury 1986, 16
16 Ibid, 18; Belton 2010, 28
17 *Housing in West Ham*
18 White 1848, quoted in Powell and Sainsbury 1986, 17
19 *TIWG*, no. 9, 1897, 57
20 Cox 1997, 152
21 Ibid, 162
22 Ibid
23 Belton 2010, 22
24 Banbury 1971, 270

25 *TIWG*, no. 9, 1896, 1
26 *TIWG*, no. 1, 1895, 18
27 *TIWG*, no. 26, 1901, 80–4
28 Ibid
29 *TIWG*, no. 2, 1895, 33
30 Powles 2005, 5
31 *TIWG*, no. 9, 1896, 1–2
32 *TIWG*, no. 2, 1895, 33
33 *TIWG*, no. 23, 1900, 149
34 Banbury 1971, 21
35 *TIWG*, no. 50, 1911, 40
36 *TIWG*, no. 9, 1896, 1
37 *TIWG*, no. 1, 1895, 26

38 Rutterford 2007, 74
39 Pollard 1950, 87
40 *TIWG*, no. 6, 1896, 42
41 *TIWG*, no. 1, 1895, 23
42 *TIWG*, 1901–2
43 A Hills in *TIWG*, no. 6, 1896, 41
44 *TIWG*, no. 10, 1897, 75
45 *TIWG*, no. 13, 1897, 4
46 *TIWG*, no. 1, 1895, 5
47 Ibid, 26
48 Walker 2010, 139
49 *TIWG*, no. 15, 1898, 118

CHAPTER 6

AFTER THE THAMES IRON WORKS

The plans of the buildings shown on the OS map published in 1920[1] are very similar to those shown on the previous OS map published in 1916 (Fig 100),[2] suggesting that there were not extensive alterations to the buildings and docks during the period immediately following their closure. However, it should be noted that the 1920 OS map was based on revisions made 1913–15, so really only describes the period immediately following the sale of the yard. The site was purchased by the Great Eastern Railway, although it is not clear for how long, if at all, they used any of the facilities on the premises. A solitary rail line can be seen on the 1914 OS map newly extending into the yard from the north and arcing over to the foundry building; this may mean that this building was maintained for a while at least (Fig 100). Alternatively, the line may have been implemented to transport machinery out of the yard to be scrapped.

Largely devoid of purpose, the yard was not allowed to stand for long. Footage from a British Pathé film of 1927, entitled *Greater London docks expansion*,[3] suggests that the dry docks in the southern portion of the yard were earmarked for a time at the end of the 1920s as ship repair facilities, although it is unclear whether any ships were ever repaired there. In the background of the footage, the ironworks appears to have been levelled. Aerial photographs taken of the site on the Essex bank in the early 1930s show the area cleared of almost all traces of the ironworks except in its most southern portion (Fig 101). The landmark engineering building survived well into the 1930s fronting the Thames (Fig 102), though what the owners (by now the London and North Eastern Railway into which the Great Eastern Railway had been grouped in 1923) used the building for is not known. The rest of the site clearly remained idle. The interwar years saw much of the former heavy industry depart from the banks of the Lea and from the East End in general. As a direct result of this, the population of West Ham, which peaked at 320,000 in the mid 1920s, dropped off sharply in the following decades, and by the early 1950s had fallen to the same level as the 1880s, despite a far greater urbanised area.[4]

The demise of heavy industry in the area was due in part to the destructive effects of continued industry on the River Lea itself. The Lea was diminished

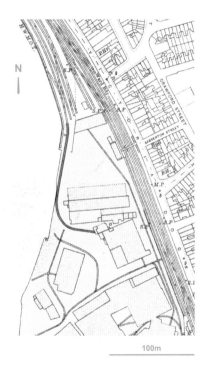

Fig 100 The 1914 OS mapping of the site; the new length of track running into the foundry building is highlighted in red (scale 1:4250)

Fig 101 Slum clearance is taking place in preparation for the new Silvertown Way Viaduct, Canning Town, in this oblique air photograph of 1933, looking north-west; the Thames Iron Works has been almost completely demolished and sidings are encroaching in the area of the southern slipways
(Historic England, epw040852)

Fig 102 The engineering building in 1938 in an oblique air photograph, looking north-east; the Silvertown Way Viaduct is complete
(Historic England, epw059407)

AFTER THE THAMES IRON WORKS

in its utility as a conduit for raw materials. However, the Lea and supply rivers and canals used in this way were becoming less important with electricity replacing coal as the provider of power to industry.[5] The loss of industry was also part of a national trend with a depressed United Kingdom economy existing for much of the late 1920s and 1930s, which, while far milder in the south-east of England than elsewhere, affected industrial areas like West Ham more severely.[6] This loss of industry was further compounded by the effects of the Blitz during the Second World War, which reduced large swathes of the area to rubble.

The engineering building had disappeared by the time of the 1950–1 OS map.[7] A map showing the distribution of Second World War bombing (Fig 103) shows a high explosive blast in the same location of the building. If the building had not previously been demolished, it seems likely that this wartime blast, as with so much of the previous life of West Ham and the East End, would mark the final chapter in the Thames Iron Works.

Beginning in the 1980s, the East End has been subject to massive regeneration and redevelopment. Derelict docks and disused industrial sites have been transformed into internationally important financial centres and desirable residential developments. Much new infrastructure has been constructed to stimulate these areas, the most significant of which are the Jubilee Line Extension, the Docklands Light Railway and now Crossrail. Despite the extensive redevelopment, the Limmo Peninsula, however, seems to have been until recently a forgotten corner of this part of London. By the mid 1980s, only a small portion of the site was still used for railway sidings and the largely fallow area subsequently became a dumping ground for earth excavated during the construction of the Docklands Light Railway, which was built over the east part of the former Thames Iron Works site. This dumped earth was encountered during the archaeological investigations and was in places several metres thick. The Crossrail project will make Canning Town an important transport hub and it is intended that the rest of the Limmo Peninsula site will be developed for mixed use, returning people again to this once thriving part of the City.

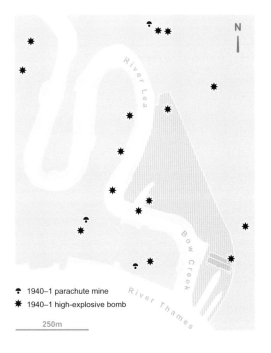

Fig 103 Second World War bombing in the area of the former Thames Iron Works (after *Scarab Close*) (scale 1:12,500)

- ⚲ 1940–1 parachute mine
- ✸ 1940–1 high-explosive bomb

250m

Notes to Chapter 6

1   OS 1913–15 [published 1920]

2   OS 1914 [published 1916]

3   British Pathé Films 1927

4   Powell and Sainsbury 1986, 15

5   Clifford 2012, 56

6   Richardson 1969, 10

7   OS 1950–1 [published 1952]

THE THAMES IRON WORKS 1837–1912

BIBLIOGRAPHY

Manuscript sources

General Register Office, London (GRO)

Births and Christenings, England   Select Births and Christenings, Provo, Utah, USA, available online @ www.ancestry.co.uk as England, Select Births and Christenings, 1538–1975

Christening Records, England and Wales   Christening Records, Provo, Utah, USA, available online @ www.ancestry.co.uk as England and Wales Christening Records, 1530–1906

Glamorgan Archives (GA)

GB 214 D179   Brown Lenox and Co Ltd records

London Metropolitan Archives (formerly Greater London Record Office) (LMA)

ACC/1712/108   deed poll Thames Iron Works and Shipbuilding Co Ltd and its liquidators and the Thames Iron Works, Shipbuilding and Engineering Co Ltd

ACC/2423/X/289   map of navigation and river from the Thames (at Limehouse and Bow Creek) to Lea Bridge: Part 2, Bow Creek to Four Mills (sheet 16), 1848–52

O/045   minute book of the Thames Iron Works and Shipbuilding and Engineering Co Ltd, 30 October 1899–14 June 1911

P87/JNE1, item 8   Saint John the Evangelist, Paddington, Register of marriages, 163

P93/DUN/73   marriages in the parish of St Dunstan, Stepney, 1568–1986

National Maritime Museum, Greenwich (NMM)

629.12   Thames Iron Works

    TIWG (*Thames Iron Works Gazette*) 14 and 15, 1898

    Excerpt from prospectus of the Thames Iron Works and Ship Building Co Ltd, archive of memorandum and articles of association, 1863

Science Museum Library and Archive Collections, London (SM)

MS 616/1   Thames Iron Works historical catalogue prepared for the Festival of Empire, Crystal Palace, 1911

The National Archives, London (TNA)

BOARD OF TRADE: COMPANIES REGISTRATION OFFICE: FILES OF DISSOLVED COMPANIES

BT 31/219/686   formation of Thames Iron Works, 1857

BT 31/913/1080C   company no. 1080C: Thames Iron Works Shipbuilding Engineering and Dry Dock Co Ltd; incorporated in 1864, dissolved before 1916, 1864–[1916]

BT 31/1597/5338   company no. 5338: Thames Ship Building Graving Docks and Iron Works Co Ltd; incorporated in 1871, dissolved before 1916, 1871–[1916]

BT 31/1722/6293   company no. 6293: Thames Iron Works and Ship Building Co Ltd; incorporated in 1872, dissolved before 1916, 1872–[1916]

BOARD OF TRADE AND SUCCESSORS: MARINE MAPS AND PLANS

BT 356/11536   map of proposed embankment for Thames Iron Works Co, 1862

CENSUS RETURNS

1841 England Census   available online @www.ancestry.co.uk

1861 England Census   available online @www.ancestry.co.uk

1871 England Census   available online @www.ancestry.co.uk

TITHE COMMISSION AND SUCCESSORS

IR 29/12/154   tithe apportionment of West Ham (parish), Essex; valuation by William Henry Dean and George Trickett, 1852

IR 30/12/154   tithe map of West Ham (parish), Essex, by ? William Dean, Stratford, 1852

Printed and other secondary works

Arnold, A J, 2000   *Iron shipbuilding on the Thames, 1832–1915: an economic and business history*, Aldershot

Banbury, P, 1971   *Shipbuilders of the Thames and Medway*, Newton Abbot

Banking almanac, 1856   The estate of Messrs C J Mare and Co, in *The banking almanac, directory, yearbook and diary for 1856* (ed D Morier Evans), 50–2, London

Barry, P, 1863a   *Dockyard economy and naval power*, London

Barry, P, 1863b   *The dockyards and the private shipyards of the kingdom*, London

Belton, B, 2010   *Founded on iron: Thames Iron Works and the origins of West Ham United*, Stroud

Bowen, F C, 1945   Shipbuilders of other days: the Thames Iron Works, *Shipbuilding Shipping Rec* 22, 375–6

Bradney Chain and Engineering Company, 1987   *A practical guide to the mooring and anchoring of small boats*, Dudley

British Pathé Films, 1927   Greater London docks expansion, http://www.british-Pathé.com/video/greater-london-docks-expansion/query/canning+town (last accessed 8 January 2014)

Brown, R J (ed), 1933   How biggest ship was safely launched, *Popular Sci Monthly* 122(2), [whole issue]

Builder, 1853   *Builder*, 17 December

Buxton, I, 2004   Some Thames and Medway dry docks, in *Shipbuilding on the Thames and Thames-built ships: proceedings of a second symposium, Greenwich, 15 February 2003* (ed R Owen), 157–70, West Wickham

Buxton, I, 2012   The output of the Thames-side yards from 1850 to 1914, in *Shipbuilding and ships on the Thames: proceedings of the fourth symposium, held 28 February 2009 at Museum of London Docklands* (ed R Owen), 132–9, West Wickham

Byrne, O, 1864   *The practical metalworker's assistant*, Philadelphia

Charles John Mare   Grace's guide: Charles John Mare, http://www.gracesguide.co.uk/Charles_John_Mare (last accessed 2 February 2015)

Cherry, B, O'Brien, C, and Pevsner, N, 2005   *The buildings of England, London: Vol 5, East*, London

Clifford, J, 2011   A wetland suburb on the edge of London: a social and environmental history of West Ham and the River Lea, 1855–1914, unpub PhD, Dept Hist York Univ, Toronto

Clifford, J, 2012   The River Lea in West Ham, in *Urban rivers* (eds S Castonguay and M Evenden), 34–56, Pittsburgh

Colledge, J J, and Warlow, B, 2010   *Ships of the Royal Navy: the complete record of all fighting ships from the Royal Navy*, Newbury

Cox, J, 1997   *London's East End: life and traditions*, London

Crouch, A P, 1900   *Silvertown and neighbourhood (including East and West Ham)*, London

Currency converter   The National Archives: currency converter [for years 1850, 1900–10], http://www.nationalarchives.gov.uk/currency (last accessed 9 February 2015)

Dawn's genealogy page [Potter family]   http://freepages.genealogy.rootsweb.ancestry.com/~dawnellis/p1444.htm (last accessed 18 February 2014)

Dickens, C, 1857   Londoners over the border, *Household Words* 16(390), 12 September, 241–4 (consulted at http://www.londonurbanvisits.co.uk/reading-2/, last accessed 2 February 2015)

Dickens, C, 2009   *The Pickwick papers* (2 vols), Newcastle

Dodd, G, 1858a   *Curiosities of industry* (16 parts, each numbered separately), London

Dodd, G, 1858b   Part 2: iron and its manufacture, in Dodd 1858a, 1–24

Dodd, G, 1858c   Part 12: a ship in the 19th century, in Dodd 1858a, 1–24

Dodd, G, 1867   *Railways, steamers and telegraphs: a glance at their recent progress and present state*, London

Dwyer, E, 2011   *The impact of the railways in the East End 1835–2010: historical archaeology from the London Overground East London line*, MOLA Monogr Ser 52, London

Edward, G, and Howarth, M A, 1907   *West Ham: a study in social and industrial problems*, Rep Outer London Inquiry Comm, London

Engineer, 1870   Thomas Ditchburn, *Engineer*, 29 April, 265 (consulted at http://www.gracesguide.co.uk/The_Engineer_1870/04/29, last accessed 4 February 2015)

Engineer, 1895   The Thames Ironworks and Shipbuilding Company, *Engineer*, 13 December, 567–77

Evans, D, 2004   *Building the steam navy*, London

Falkirk C T   Falkirk community trust, http://collections.falkirk.gov.uk/search.do;jsessionid=CEB5D34CA7223DAFEF729899BFEB5?id=24032&db=person&view=detail& mode=1 (last accessed 23 July 2014)

Gardens of Alcatraz   The gardens of Alcatraz: building block of history, http://alcatrazgardens.org/blog/index.php/2011/07/building-blocks-of-history/ (last accessed 23 July 2014)

General steam   Grace's guide: General Steam Navigation Co, http://www.gracesguide.co.uk/General_Steam_Navigation_Co (last accessed 9 January 2015)

Hansard   Hansard 1803–2005, http://hansard.millbanksystems.com (last accessed 18 February 2015)

Hartshorne, H, 1881   *The household cyclopedia of general information*, New York

Hill, A, 2001   *The South Yorkshire coalfield: a history and development*, Stroud

Hills, A F, 1911   *Causes of the Thames Iron Works collapse* [pamphlet], London

HMS Rattler   Memorials and monuments in Portsmouth: Portsmouth's historic dockyard – HMS *Rattler*, http://www.memorials.inportsmouth.co.uk/dockyard/rattler.htm (last accessed 31 July 2014)

Housing in West Ham   The Newham story: housing in West Ham, http://www.newhamstory.com/node/1820 (last accessed 11 April 2014)

ILN   *Illustrated London News*, 1845–66 [selected years] (consulted online at British Library)

ILN 1854   Iron shipbuilding at Blackwall, *ILN* 28 October, 409–10

Jackson, A A, 1978   *London's local railways*, Newton Abbot

Jobling, H J W, 1993   The history and development of English anchors *c* 1550 to 1850, unpub MA dissertation, Texas Univ

John Readhead's shipyard   John Readhead's shipyard index, http://www.bagejohn.webspace.virginmedia.com/JohnReadheadShipyard%20Page24.htm (last accessed 23 July 2014)

The lads in the shipyard   RMS *Titanic* remembered: the lads in the shipyard, http://www.rmstitanicremembered.com/?page_id=107 (last accessed 23 July 2014)

Landes, D S, 1969   *The unbound Prometheus: technological change and industrial development in western Europe from 1750 to the present*, Cambridge

LCC   London County Council, 1994a Blackwall Yard: development, to *c* 1819, in *Poplar, Blackwall and the Isle of Dogs: the parish of All Saints* (ed S Porter, gen ed H Hobhouse), Survey of London 43–4, 553–65, London (consulted at http://www.british-history.ac.uk/survey-london/vols43-4/pp553-565, last accessed 7 January 2015)

LCC   London County Council, 1994b *Poplar, Blackwall and the Isle of Dogs: the parish of All Saints* (ed S Porter, gen ed H Hobhouse), Survey of London 43–4, London

Lewis, J, 1999   *London's Lea valley*, Chichester

Mackrow, G C, 1900   The Cleopatra Needle or obelisk (illustrated), *Thames Iron Works Q Gazette* 4(23) (June), 111–15 (consulted at http://www.jstor.org/discover/10.2307/60226676, last accessed 2 February 2015)

Marshall, G, 2013   *London's industrial heritage*, Stroud

Mechanics' Mag, 1861   Leviathan workshops no. 1, *Mechanics' Mag* 6 ns, 138, 94–6

Miall, C M, 1893   Cyclops in London, *Cornhill Mag* 67 os, 20 ns, 170–7

Miles, E, with Miles, L, 1841   *An epitome, historical and statistical, descriptive of the Royal Naval Service of England*, London

Mould, Q, 1997   Leather, in Hawkes, J W, and Fasham, P J, *Excavations on Reading waterfront sites, 1979–88*, Wessex Archaeol Rep 5, 108–42, Salisbury

Mould loft   The loftsman [Leith shipyards]: the mould loft, http://www.leithshipyards.com/mould-loft/lofting.html (last accessed 18 February 2015)

Murphy, H, Johnman, L, and Ritchie, A, 1988 Deaccessioning and British shipbuilding records, in *Proceedings of the annual conference 1997 of the Business Archives Council* (ed L M Richmond), 159–85, London

Museum of London, 1994 (1990)   *Archaeological site manual*, 3 edn, London

Museum of London, 2002   *A research framework for London archaeology 2002*, London

Nasmyth, J, and Smiles, S, 1883   *James Nasmyth engineer: an autobiography*, London

OS, 1867   Ordnance Survey, *First edition 25 inch to the mile: London sheet XXXVIII; London sheet XLVII* [surveyed 1867, published 1869], London

OS, 1894   Ordnance Survey, *Second edition 25 inch to the mile: London sheet LXV/Middlesex sheet XVIII, 9; London sheet LXXIX/Middlesex sheet XVIII, 13* [surveyed 1894, published 1897], London

OS, 1913–15   Ordnance Survey, *Six inches to the mile: London sheet L* [surveyed 1913–15, published 1920], London

OS, 1914   Ordnance Survey, *Third edition 25 inch to the mile: London sheet VI, 9/Essex ns sheet nLXXXVI, 9; London sheet VI, 13/Essex ns sheet nLXXXVI, 13* [surveyed 1914, published 1916], London

OS, 1950–1   Ordnance Survey, *25 inch London and environs (1:2500)* [surveyed 1950–1, published 1952], Southampton

P&O heritage   P&O heritage: General Steam Navigation Company, http://www.poheritage.com/our-history/company-guides/general-steam-navigation-company/NextPage?pageIndex=2 (last accessed 9 January 2015)

Piwarzyk, R W, 1996   The bricks of Santa Cruz, in The Laguna limekilns: Bonny Doon, unpub MS (consulted at http://scplweb.santacruzpl.org/history/work/limebric.shtml, last accessed 23 July 2014)

Pollard, S, 1950   The decline of shipbuilding on the Thames, *Econ Hist Rev*, ns 3(1), 72–89

Pollard, S, 1957   British and world shipbuilding, 1890–1914: a study in comparative costs, *J Econ Hist* 17, 426–44

Powell, W R (ed), and Sainsbury, F, 1986   *West Ham 1886–1986*, London

Powles, J, 2005   *Iron in the blood*, Nottingham

Rankin, J, 2014   De La Rue seals deal to print plastic UK banknotes, *Guardian*, 8 September 2014 (consulted at http://www.theguardian.com/business/2014/sep/08/de-la-rue-seals-deal-plastic-uk-banknotes, last accessed 3 February 2015)

Reed, E J, 1869   *Shipbuilding in iron and steel*, London

Richardson, H W, 1969   The Great Depression, *J Contemporary Hist* 4(4), 3–19

Royal Victoria Dock   Royal docks trust: Royal Victoria Dock, http://www.royaldockstrust.org.uk (last accessed 19 February 2015)

Russell, J S, 1845   *Report on waves: made to the meetings of the British Association in 1842–3*, London

Rutterford, J, 2007   Thames iron: history of a new issue, in *Shipbuilding and ships on the Thames: proceedings of the third symposium, held on 18 February 2006 at Greenwich Maritime Institute, Old Royal Naval College, Greenwich* (ed R Owen), 73–90, West Wickham

Scarab Close   Bomb sight: high explosive bomb at Scarab Close, http://bombsight.org/bombs/8816/ (last accessed 18 February 2015)

Ships list a   http://www.theshipslist.com/ships/lines/generalscrewssc.shtml (last accessed 23 July 2014)

Ships list b   http://www.theshipslist.com/ships/lines/royalmail.shtml (last accessed 23 July 2014)

Slaven, A, 1980   The shipbuilding industry, in *The dynamics of Victorian business* (ed R Church), 107–25, London

Smith, E C, 1924   Thames steam pioneers: the iron shipbuilders, *Lloyd's list* 26 March, pages not available

Smith, T P, 2005   The materials used to build the kilns, in Tyler, K, with Brown, J, Smith, T P, and Whittingham, L, *The Doulton stoneware pothouse in Lambeth: excavations at 9 Albert Embankment, London*, MoLAS Archaeol Stud Ser 15, 32–6, London

Swann, J, 1982   *Shoes*, London

Thames Iron Works   Port cities London: Thames Iron Works, http://www.portcities.org.uk/london/server/show/ConNarrative.59/chapterId/1030/Thames-Ironworks.html (accessed 11 April 2014)

The Times   *Times Digital Archive*, 1785–2006, Gale Cengage Learning, gale.cengage.co.uk (last accessed 23 July 2014)

TIWG   *Thames Iron Works Gazette* (quarterly, 1895–1911) (consulted at National Maritime Museum)

Timbs, J (ed), 1840   The London and Blackwall railway, *Literary World* 3(68), 225–7

VCH, 1907   *The Victoria history of the county of Essex: Vol 2* (eds W Page and J H Round), London

Walker, F, 2010   *Ships and shipbuilders*, Barnsley

Weissenbacher, M, 2009   *Sources of power: how energy forges human history* (2 vols), Santa Barbara

Wells, J, 1987   *The immortal* Warrior*: Britain's first and last battleship*, Emsworth

White, W, 1848   *History, gazetteer and directory of the county of Essex*, Sheffield